Maria

REVISED AND
EXPANDED EDITION

Maria

by Richard L. Spivey

🌿 Northland Publishing

in memory of

POPOVI DA

Publisher's note: Ownership credits, where indicated, reflect the status at the time of the original printing (1979); due to the passage of time and the nature of collecting, however, these credits are not necessarily correct at this printing.

Frontispiece: Black-on-black plate (1967); feather design, 11¾" diameter. Signature: Maria/Popovi 467. Private Collection. Photograph by Jerry Jacka.

Page 127: Polychrome jar, curvilinear designs floral motif, 7½" × 11". Unsigned. Dated c. 1920 by K. M. Chapman. School of American Research Catalog No. IAF 1354. Courtesy School of American Research, Santa Fe, New Mexico.

Copyright © 1979 by Richard Spivey
All Rights Reserved
SECOND EDITION, JULY 1989
Second Printing, October 1989
ISBN 0-87358-499-6 Cloth
ISBN 0-87358-484-8 Softcover
Library of Congress Catalog Card Number 78-71373
Composed and Printed in the United States of America

CONTENTS

ILLUSTRATIONS

Pottery and Signatures

vi

People, Places, and Processes

viii

FOREWORD

Much of the American Southwest's Indian art is nameless. It was conceived in a past without written record and surrendered to an on-rushing Anglo culture without documentation. Far too often one reads "Anonymous" on a museum exhibit label opposite a kachina doll, textile, basket, silver bracelet, or painted ceramic.

Perhaps more than any other artist, Maria Martinez of San Ildefonso Pueblo, brought "signatures" to Indian art. She and other members of her family revived a dying art form and kindled a renaissance in pottery for all of the Pueblos. By her own artistic example she raised this regional art to one of international acclaim.

In recent years much has been written about Southwestern pottery. Maria herself is the subject of numerous books and articles. Each in its fashion has made a contribution to our knowledge and appreciation of her art. Unfortunately none has sought to present the full range of her art. That is the aim of this book.

Richard Spivey is a personal friend of the Martinez family and an acknowledged authority on contemporary Pueblo pottery. His text is an important statement on Maria and her art.

Jerry Jacka was the natural choice to photograph the art of the Martinez family. A pottery collector himself, Jerry brings to his work a reverence for Indian art. His art photography has long been associated with *Arizona Highways* and *American Indian Art Magazine*.

Laura Gilpin, one of the Southwest's greatest photographers, and a longtime friend of Maria, has provided many historic photographs to illustrate the text.

Since my first exposure to Pueblo pottery in 1970, my interest in the Martinez family has never waned. In fact, my appreciation of their art has increased as has my affection and respect. It is my hope that this book will stir others to this appreciation of the Martinez tradition in Pueblo pottery.

Long may it live!

DENNIS LYON
Scottsdale, Arizona

ix

Maria. Photograph by Cradoc Bagshaw.

PREFACE TO THE
REVISED EDITION

Because of the death of Maria, it is with a certain sadness that I approached the task of working on a revised edition of *Maria*. The pleasure of working with Maria was foremost in writing the original manuscript. That would not happen again. Maria died on July 20, 1980. Prior to her death, I had the privilege of being guest curator at the Wheelwright Museum of the American Indian in Santa Fe for a major Maria retrospective. I was excited about the prospect of Maria seeing so many of her best pieces assembled in one exhibit. Sadly, because of failing health, Maria never got to see the retrospective. However, when I went to San Ildefonso Pueblo to tell her how wonderful it was to have such a grand display of her work and to tell her about the exhibit, she responded, "I don't have to see those pots; I've seen them all before."

Tony Da was seriously injured in a motorcycle accident in 1982, which left him with a twenty-five-year memory loss and a partial disability. He has since returned to painting, working in a style reminiscent of his earlier watercolors, but simpler and in brighter tones. It is highly unlikely that he will return to pottery-making again.

I had a particular purpose in mind in writing the original volume, which I felt had been accomplished. Therefore, it was decided not to make any changes in the original book, but to add a new chapter. The purpose of the new chapter is to add new information, expand old information, to make some corrections, and to belabor the point that Maria's early work were simple pieces in Polychrome, and not, as so many other writers and museum catalogs and exhibitions have stated, Blackware or Black-on-black ware encouraged by Edgar L. Hewett.

The original preface stands, as those whom I thanked before, I continue to thank. In addition, in the preparation of the revised edition I owe a debt of gratitude to Nancy Fox, Senior Curator of Collections at the

Museum of Indian Arts and Culture/Laboratory of Anthropology, Museum of New Mexico; Dr. Patrick Houlihan, Director of the Millicent Rogers Museum, Taos, New Mexico; Michael Herring, Director of the Indian Arts Research Center at the School of American Research, Santa Fe; also at the School of American Research: Lynn Brittner, curator, Tara Travis, administrative assistant, and Eunice Kahn, museum aide. Again my good friend, Richard M. Howard, has given invaluable help. My sister, Glenda Spivey Fabre, translated portions of Edgar L. Hewett's *Les Communantés Anciennes dans le Désert Américain* from the original French. I am deeply indebted to Marjorie F. Lambert, for reading the portions of the manuscript relating to Pajaritan pottery. Blue Corn, Mrs. John Gaw Meem, Letta Wofford, Marjory and Victor Hansen, Margaret Lou Gutierrez, Tomasita Montoya Sanchez, and the staff at the Carmel Public Library were all of great assistance. Jerry Jacka and Herb Lotz have provided some fine new photographs. Anita Da was always available and of never-ending help, as she was before. I thank my wife Lynne for constant encouragement. And finally, a special recognition has to go to Dennis Lyon, whose enthusiasm and love of Maria's pottery led to the book in the first place.

PREFACE

This book is not intended to be a biography of Maria Martinez, since her life has been well-covered by Alice Marriott in *María: The Potter of San Ildefonso*. Nor is it intended to be a technical exposition on pottery making at San Ildefonso Pueblo, since that has been done by Carl E. Guthe in his detailed and technical study, *Pueblo Pottery Making: A Study at the Village of San Ildefonso;* by Marjorie F. Lambert in her briefer but excellent publication, *Pueblo Pottery Making: Materials, Tools, and Techniques;* and by Kenneth M. Chapman in his definitive study, *The Pottery of San Ildefonso Pueblo.*

Maria is the most famous Indian artist of all time. This book traces the development of Maria's pottery over the span of some seventy years of her career, capturing something of the essence of Maria as a person and presenting her work as a timeless art form.

In reality there is a second text running through this publication. Many of the captions for the photographs are statements by Maria herself, which were obtained from a series of conversations with the author during the winter, spring, and summer of 1977. These quotations work independently from the text; Maria directly tells part of her own story and at the same time indirectly gives insight into her personality and character. I have taken the liberty of editing these quotations to a limited degree since English is Maria's third language. The other two are Tewa, her mother tongue, and Spanish, which she speaks fluently.

I am deeply indebted to Maria's son, Popovi Da; without him this book would never have been written. When I first came to New Mexico it was Po who encouraged and helped to involve me with Pueblo Indian pottery. He was my mentor and close personal friend. His death in October, 1971, was a great personal loss. Appropriately, the introduction is a statement by Po himself making a correlation of Indian cultural values with Indian art.

Anita Da, Po's wife, has worked closely with me in gathering the material for *María*. She has given freely of her personal knowledge and granted me access to her files and to the museum at the Popovi Da Studio in San Ildefonso. Anita, thank you.

There have been so many others who have helped, encouraged, and supported this project that a complete list would be a long one. Jerry Jacka has taken so many marvelous photographs at so many times and so many places. Laura Gilpin has graciously opened her archives allowing us to use whichever photographs we wished. Photographer Cradoc Bagshaw not only photographed for this book, but kindly lent a light box, the use of which has proven invaluable for working with the photographic transparencies.

Special thanks go to: Betty Toulouse and Nancy Fox, Curators of Collections at the Laboratory of Anthropology, Museum of New Mexico, both of whom graciously allowed me almost unrestricted access to the files and collections at the Laboratory; Edna Robertson, Curator of Collections at the Museum of Fine Arts at the Museum of New Mexico and Arthur H. Wolf, Curator of Collections at the School of American Research, who opened the doors to the Indian Arts Fund Collection; Dr. Douglas Schwartz, Director of the School of American Research; Nora Fisher, Museum of International Folk Art, Santa Fe; Art Olivas, Curator of Photo Archives, History Division, Museum of New Mexico; and Laura Michael and Margo Lamb, librarians at the Laboratory of Anthropology, Museum of New Mexico, who greatly helped in gathering resource materials from diverse sources; and Dr. Patrick Houlihan, Director of the Heard Museum in Phoenix, Arizona, who kindly gave us access to that museum's collections.

I should like to acknowledge other debts: to my good friends Janis Lyon and Barbara Rolita who gave up vacation time to help collect data on some of the pottery shown here; to friends Sally Kandarian, Gilbert Atencio, Sallie Wagner, Marie Varenhorst, Letta Wofford, Peter Waidler, John L. Lenssen, Mark Bahti, Harry O. King, Jr., Dr. and Mrs. Edward Cook, Dr. Helen Wilson, Clara Lee Tanner, and Richard Mallory; to Shirley Taylor who typed the manuscript; and to two special friends whose names I cannot mention; and to all the collectors who so graciously opened their homes to allow their collections to be photographed, I wish to extend a collective thank you.

My sister Glenda Spivey Fabre gave editorial help and inspiration.

Marjorie F. Lambert, Richard M. Howard, and Dr. Patrick Houlihan gave of their time to read the manuscript critically; their help was invaluable.

And most of all, my thanks to Maria Martinez, who at age ninety remains indefatigable. Working with her always will remain one of the great experiences of my life.

RICHARD L. SPIVEY
Santa Fe, New Mexico

Well, I like the polychrome very much because that's the first we made.
And the black later on we made.

MARIA

Popovi Da. Photograph by Laura Gilpin.

INDIAN POTTERY
AND INDIAN VALUES*1

by Popovi Da

I stand before you, ladies and gentlemen, as an Indian, at this moment, to speak about our pottery, our tradition, and our culture. Our culture and within it our creative arts are woven and inseparable. Everything in our life is all-inclusive. We must preserve what has been created and what can be created. The force continues. . . .

Time is the limiting factor in the endless spirit of our people that shortens what I have to say. Indeed, the clockwork time which you have invented can be disastrous. And there is another matter which disturbs me: the way that we are often treated as academic curiosities. This indeed is sad. You have written too many books and papers about us without having the experience of the feeling within us.

We believe we are the first conservationists. We do not destroy or disturb the harmony of nature. To us this is beauty; it is our sense of esthetics. We care for and husband our environment, trying to be all-forbearing like Mother Earth. We feel ourselves trustees of our environment and of our creative values. And this gives us a union with all existence, all the creatures which live in the world: wild animals, little crawling things, and even men.

We have multitudes of symbols — corn blossom, squash blossom, eagle and deer, rainbow and fire, and storm cloud; the design of plants, of all living things; the underworld which gave forth man and all the creatures — symbols whose secret meanings are only secret because they are within and cannot be easily expressed. This symbolism is perpetuated through memory alone, because we have no written language. But to be able to use our symbols and keep in harmony with our world we must

*A talk given by Popovi Da as a part of the School of American Research lecture series in December, 1969.

Popovi Da's hands. Photograph by Laura Gilpin.

work by fasting, continence, solitary vigil, and symbolic discipline. Out of the silences of meditation come purity and power which eventually become apparent in our art: the many spirits which enter about us, in us, are transformed within us, moving from an endless past not gone, not dead, but with a threshold that is the present. From this time sense, from this experience deep within, our forms are created. Even our smaller children sense this, and consequently create beautiful designs. Our simple lines have meaning.

We do what comes from thinking, and sometimes hours and even days are spent to create an esthetic scroll in a design.

Our symbols and our ceremonial representations are all expressed as an endless cadence, and beautifully organized in our art as well as in our dance.

A pueblo dance is a sacred drama and a tremendous religious experience to us. You behold a masterpiece of color, form and movement, sound, rhythm, a slow sequence of chants, beat of feet. This ceremony combines our spiritual and our physical needs. The dance expresses the union we feel between man and the whole of humanity or the union of all living things. At the same time, the dance gives to man, in his trusteeship of the corn, the health of the plant. The dance encourages the corn to grow.

In our pottery we have many distinctive styles within historic periods. As our society changed throughout the ages, there appeared variations in our art related to the life of the people. In time of high prosperity, pottery styles and our artistic talents were directed to forms showing our affluence: detailed lines, fine in form and of many colors and styles. Abundant harvests called for new original creations. The years when our culture was appreciated by those in power resulted in a more adequate life for all of us, and this life was reflected in our art by intricate patterns in design, in basketry, painting, and petroglyphic drawings.

During droughts and periods of trouble, we created less than at other times. This was not due, as is often believed, to the lack of facilities, but because these were periods of oppression and frustration when the mind was controlled by anxiety.

Fine art within our lives has been balanced and directed in a positive sense by the forces about us. If life is unbalanced, as it is now, by the pressure of mechanical things all about us, life seems to lose man in a cold world of steel where we are frustrated and afraid. This frustration will be reflected in our art. Should our civilization terminate today, future anthropologists would be puzzled by finding in our pueblos Japanese artifacts, complex distorted patterns of abstract paintings, and other evidence of the confusion of the world about us.

Popovi Da's hands. Photograph by Laura Gilpin.

But the best in pueblo life is reflected by paintings and designs which tend to be four-dimensional. They point to rhythm and the motion in the dance, the action of the horse, the speed of the antelope, the heat of the desert. We have a form of art which is distinctively North American Indian, and we must preserve our way of life in order for our art to continue. From this part of us comes our ability to create, as can be seen from the thousands of designs found on ceremonial and cooking pots from prehistory, dating back to time immemorial. I doubt that the designs improved the cooking, but they were created because they had to be created; it is our role to create.

Except for our ritualistic dances and our way of life, our efforts are related to the care of our environment and what we create. Our pueblo people eat gently, recognizing with inner feelings that the corn or the squash were at one time growing, cared for, each a plant alive, now prepared to become part of us, of our bodies and our minds, quite sacred. We reflect on the plant.

Now let me point a finger at you. You buy a can of corn or squash at the supermarket. The cans are cans, the names "corn" and "squash" things on the shelf, moribund. You even have powdered potatoes: you don't even know how they grow or the designs that these plants can create within the mind. You have withdrawn from the basic natural environment, from what we look upon as reality.

There is a design in living things; their shapes, forms, the ability to live, all have meaning. We must cling to our Indian traditions which exalt beauty. To the white man, religion is a method, a system which he can employ or even use at times when necessary. But to us there is no word in our language for an isolated dogma: all we can say is that we have a way of life, and that this is life itself. If we fill our minds with pure materialism and accept a convenient religion, then the backbone of our way of life, of our perception of beauty, will be broken and we will disappear as unseen winds, gone. You, too, are not secure. You may be the victims of your own dissolution, undermined by customs, air pollution, in fact by unremovable pollution of all kinds, material and spiritual. You can come to us for our message. We must not let ourselves get caught up in the onrushing vanishing years or the results of an over-efficient society, highly mechanized, streamlined, rapidly moving at a rate and in a way that to most of the Indians represents a panic.

The State government will try to gain our land through condemnation. The Federal government will try to take land for parks and forest services. There will be no feeling for the great trust we have in the land. What will happen to Blue Lake* and other sacred areas?

Our values are indwelling and dependent on time and space unmeasured. This in itself is beauty. Our first great value is our trusteeship of nature, and this is beauty also. Then there is an order and direction of our lives, a unity, the ability to share the joy of sharing, creativeness and minimum competition. This too is beauty.

Come to our dances or our homes; we share our meals with you. We feel then that we can be part of each other, confluent human forces, sharing giving. It is not the disease known as obligation, but exists because it exists and that is enough.

---

*Blue Lake was returned to Taos Pueblo in 1971.

Maria with her pottery from the collections of the School of American Research and the Museum of New Mexico (1976). Photograph by Jerry Jacka.

CHAPTER ONE

Maria

M ARIA, THE POTTER OF SAN ILDEFONSO, is not only the most famous of Pueblo Indian potters, but she also ranks among the best of international potters. Her work is exhibited in museums and private collections throughout the world. She is one of those rare people who, when their acquired skills work in harmony with their innate artistic abilities, leave the world all the richer for their presence. Maria is an artist.

But Maria is more. From her own point of view, she is a Pueblo Indian woman; nothing more, nothing less. She lives a simple life as those before her have always lived a simple life. The Pueblo Indian views life as an integrated whole; and all of the parts, working together in harmony, have their place within this whole: family, community, religion, culture, living and dying. Until recently, individual achievement has been a foreign idea to this culture. An individual did not excel; the group excelled. Maria belongs to and is a part of her culture, religion, pueblo, and family. They come first; they have to come first. But there is no conflict. Pueblo Indian ceremonial life is everyday life. This is the way Maria has always lived, and this is the way she has always wanted to live. Alice Marriott, in her well known biography of Maria, writes, "The most striking characteristic I have found in Mrs. Martinez, however, is that she does not regard herself as an exception to the general rule. Her life has been, as nearly as she could make it, the normal life of a woman of her culture."[1] Maria is a wife, mother, and wholly a member of the Pueblo community.

But Maria is more. When family or friends are in need of help or food or money, she gives, she shares. When she has little, she gives of what she has, saving only the smallest portion for herself. When Maria attained skills as a potter that gave her a considerable edge over the other

Maria. Photograph by Cradoc Bagshaw.

potters, she shared those skills. Maria is, in the fullest sense of the term, a human being.

Her life has not been an easy one; she has had to work for whatever she earned. She worked long hours, days, and years to develop her pottery skills. She had her family to raise and care for. She had her community and ceremonial obligations, which she took seriously. She has lost a husband and three sons. Yet each time Maria surmounted these tragedies. Maria has strength, spirit, and character.

She is humble, proud, sometimes reserved, yet outgoing, friendly, and gregarious. She loves people and people love her. She feels the reason that people love her is that she first loves them. She never turns a friend away from her door. Her heart is always open.

But Maria is more. She is surrounded by that particular aura reflecting both inner beauty and greatness. When you are in her presence, you might first feel awe knowing who and what she is, though very soon you will feel comfortable because of the warmth she radiates. Still, you know you are in the presence of someone unique, very special.

Throughout her long career, Maria's dedication to her work has been paramount. By her inspiration and example, and by her sharing and teaching, she revived a dying art and led a Pueblo economy from one of poverty to one of relative affluence. In the history of a people, on occasion a genius will come forward and lead them to new heights of artistic expression. Maria is that person.

But Maria is more. Maria is poor and she is rich. She is poor because she has little of material value. She has little because she has always given and shared. She no longer makes pottery so there is no income. But she is rich. She is rich because she has led a full and fruitful life, a good life. She has her family, her friends, and her pueblo and culture. She has her memories and accomplishments. Maria is happy.

Recent photograph of San Ildefonso Pueblo taken from one of the hills above the pueblo to the east. Immediately in the center foreground is Maria's house. The shed to the left is where Maria and Popovi Da fired in later years. The trees at the far edge of the pueblo follow the course of the Rio Grande. In the background is the Pajarito Plateau.

Photograph by Laura Gilpin

CHAPTER TWO

San Ildefonso

SAN ILDEFONSO PUEBLO, of the Tewa linguistic family, is located about twenty miles northwest of Santa Fe, New Mexico. Beautifully situated on the eastern bank of the Rio Grande between the Jemez mountain range on the west and the Sangre de Cristo Mountains on the east, it has been inhabited since about A.D. 1300. The site of the village has shifted several times, the earliest known location being about one mile from the present village. Archaeological evidence suggests that the ancestors of San Ildefonso were among the inhabitants of at least three Tewa-speaking villages located in the canyons and cliffs of the Pajarito Plateau west of the present village. Legend at San Ildefonso has it that Mesa Verde in southern Colorado is their original ancestral home. San Ildefonso was one of the most prosperous and flourishing villages in pre-Spanish times.

The village which Oñate visited in 1598 was then called *Powhoge* in the native tongue, which in Tewa means "where the water cuts through," referring to the Rio Grande. The name San Ildefonso was applied after 1617 when a mission church of that saint was established there. Following many years of oppression and religious persecution, the Rio Grande Pueblos united and drove the Spaniards from New Mexico in 1680. In 1692 De Vargas led the "bloodless reconquest," re-establishing Spanish control over the region. In 1694, not wanting to accept the reconquest, the people of San Ildefonso abandoned their homes and moved to the top of Black Mesa *(Tunyo)*, just north of the village, where for nine months they withstood three assaults by De Vargas's troops. But after the fourth assault they surrendered and returned to their homes. Two years later, because of crop failures and continued religious suppression, they abandoned the village to live with other tribes, including the Hopi in Arizona. The Spaniards resettled the village with other

COLORADO

●Mesa Verde

ARIZONA

Pajarito Plateau

Rio Grande

●San Ildefonso
●Santa Fe

NEW
MEXICO

●El Paso

MEXICO   TEXAS

The location of San Ildefonso Pueblo.

Tewa-speaking peoples by 1702. A smallpox epidemic wiped out half
the population in the late 1700s.* Religious suppression continued; San
Ildefonso was the scene of many witchcraft trials. This led to a peculiar
blend of Catholic and Tewa Indian religion: in reality, a veneer of
Christianity which still exists today.

The year 1846 saw the beginning of American occupation, recon-
firmation of the title to Pueblo lands given by royal Spanish land grants,
and subjugation of such roving tribes as the Apache, Navajo, and Ute.
The railroad was completed in 1880; a bridge was built across the Rio
Grande just west of San Ildefonso in 1924; and the city of Los Alamos
arose on the Pajarito Plateau to develop the atomic bomb during World
War II. The impact of these events is reflected in the development of
pottery styles, as we shall discuss.

Many centuries before the white man arrived, the native Pueblo
style of architecture, social organization, agriculture, religion, and artistic expression were well established.

> Many of the arts and crafts of this peaceful and industrious
> people have been carried on since early pre-Columbian times,
> and of these their pottery will stand as a supreme achieve-
> ment, comparable with the best of ceramic products of ancient

6

*The population of San Ildefonso diminished from 3000 in 1700 to 100 by 1900. The current
(1977) population is 471.

Mexico and Peru, and of Old World cultures of a similar level. But where the native ceramic art of many other lands has passed into oblivion, that of the Pueblos survives today, not as a mere utility, but by its very form and decoration embodying, as in ancient times, the best of tribal traditions.[1]

The earliest record of San Ildefonso pottery, other than passing mention in early Spanish chronicles, is that of the 1880 Smithsonian Expedition headed by James Stevenson. In his report of that expedition he lists the following articles of clay: "These consist of painted whiteware with decorations in black; polished black and brown ware."[2] He also lists a red ware with decorations in black. The production of pottery at San Ildefonso at the time of his visit was very limited:

> But few specimens were obtained here. The people of this small pueblo devote their time chiefly to agriculture and pastoral pursuits, and have almost abandoned the manufacture of pottery, that in use by them at the present time being chiefly obtained from neighboring tribes.[3]

The first detailed and technical study of pottery making was done by Carl Guthe at San Ildefonso in 1921. A major study by Chapman was published in 1970. The actual collection of representative samples of Pueblo ceramics was begun in 1923 by the Indian Arts Fund in Santa Fe, New Mexico.

Other than culinary ware, which changed very little in form over a long period of time, the earliest pottery we are concerned with here is San Ildefonso Black-on-cream ware (Figure 2.1). It dates from about 1760 and continued to be made almost exclusively until about 1880. A typical jar was globular in shape with a short, slightly flared neck; in a narrow zone on the neck and a wide zone on the body, abstract geometric motifs were painted with guaco* on a stone-polished cream slip. The rims were slipped and polished red, and a polished red band was placed immediately below the decorative field.

With the opening of the Santa Fe Trail in 1821, pottery manufacture began to decline rapidly, being replaced in the Pueblos by tin pails and enamelware containers. By 1830 ceramic output was largely limited to storage jars and a few smaller shapes. In the period 1850–1880, the extinction of pottery-making at San Ildefonso was avoided by just a few traditional potters.

---

*Guaco is a vegetal paint which turns black during firing. It is made by boiling the Rocky Mountain Bee Plant to a thick and syrupy consistency. Guaco has been used at San Ildefonso, Tesuque, Cochiti, and Santo Domingo. This paint is compatible with the bentonite clay used at these four Pueblos. In contrast, the kaolin clay used by the other Pueblos (Acoma, Laguna, Zuni, Hopi, Isleta, Santa Ana, and Zia) requires a mineral paint.

Figure 2.1   San Ildefonso Black-on-cream ware, San Ildefonso slip (c. 1875–1880); bird and floral motifs, 15½″ x 17″, unsigned. Courtesy Mr. and Mrs. Dennis Lyon, Scottsdale. Photograph by Jerry Jacka.

Figure 2.2 Black-on-red jar (c. 1900); unusual double-bellied jar done in the late 19th century style, 7¾″ x 7″. Unsigned (probably made by Dominguita Pino Martinez and painted by Alfredo Montoya). Collection of author, Santa Fe. Photograph by Cradoc Bagshaw.

Figure 2.3 San Ildefonso Polychrome storage jar, Cochiti slip (c. 1910); typical late 19th century storage jar with turkey and fish designs, 22″ x 21¾″, unsigned. Courtesy School of American Research, Indian Arts Fund, Catalog Number IAF 264. Photograph by Jerry Jacka.

10

Black-on-red ware originated about 1850; it closely resembles the Black-on-cream pottery except that a more highly stone-polished rust-red slip was used as a background for the black designs. However, Black-on-red vessels continued to be produced beyond the Black-on-cream ware. As younger potters came on the scene, there was innovation in shapes. In the early years production was minor, but during the later years there was specialization in making Black-on-red pottery by some potters, particularly Domingita Pino Martinez and her daughter, Tonita Montoya Roybal. With the death of Tonita in 1945, the production of Black-on-red pottery ceased.

Popular myth attributes the discovery of Black ware to Maria and Julian, which is not true. In fact, they discovered Black-on-black ware as will be discussed later. San Ildefonso has a long tradition of Black ware, although never as strong as that of the neighboring Tewa Pueblos of Santa Clara and San Juan. San Ildefonso Black ware was stone-polished, globular-shaped jars smoked black during firing. At San Ildefonso, Black ware had made little progress, and by the turn of the last century, even the slight production had all but ceased.[5] The Indians of San Ildefonso say they have always made polished Black ware; there is little doubt that the early Black ware specimens are actually from San Ildefonso.[6] Spinden reports Black ware still being made at San Ildefonso as late as 1911.[7]

Development of San Ildefonso Polychrome ware may have begun as early as 1875. Certainly by the early 1880s there was experimentation in the use of red on vessels which were otherwise Black-on-cream pottery. The original design elements were the same as those on Black-on-cream ware, but soon the older design elements were modified and elaborated to feature curvilinear elements and floral and bird motifs. The use of red at first was cautious, but soon it achieved a nice balance with the black.

Initially, the simpler forms continued, but by the turn of the century, the adaptation of a two-hundred-year-old form borrowed from Santa Clara predominated; this jar was more squat with a longer neck and a flaring rim — a very graceful shape (Figure 3.1). The Black-on-red ware also followed the same trends into new shapes. Shortly after 1900 the native cream slip which required vigorous stone polishing was replaced by a Cochiti slip which only required rag polishing. Unfortunately, at San Ildefonso, it was not usually handled properly. The result was often grainy, streaked, and dull grey. The polished red rim was retained until about 1910 when most potters began to paint it black. Polychrome ware continued to be made until just after 1925 and was then almost discontinued.

One would think that contact with European culture would have influenced Pueblo ceramics beginning around 1600, but

11

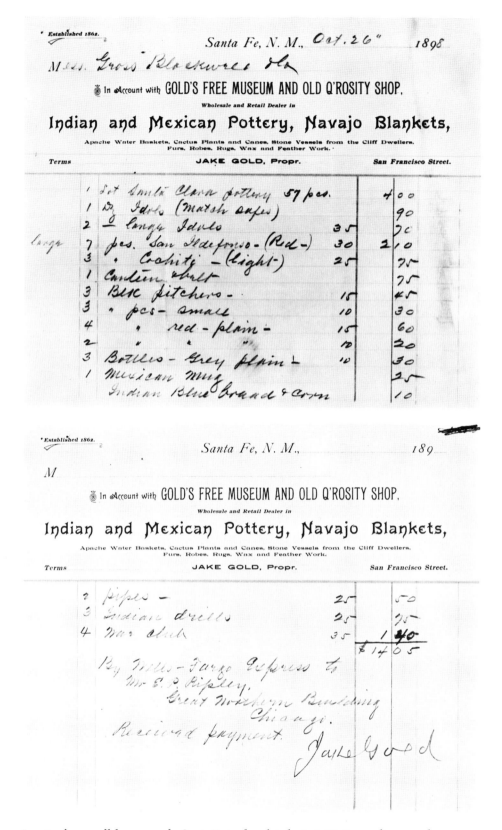

* Established 1861.

Santa Fe, N. M., *Oct. 26"* 1898

Mess. Gross Blackwell & Co.

In Account with GOLD'S FREE MUSEUM AND OLD Q'ROSITY SHOP.

Wholesale and Retail Dealer in

Indian and Mexican Pottery, Navajo Blankets,

Apache Water Baskets, Cactus Plants and Canes, Stone Vessels from the Cliff Dwellers.
Furs, Robes, Rugs, Wax and Feather Work.

Terms   JAKE GOLD, Propr.   San Francisco Street.

	1	Lot Santa Clara pottery 57 pcs.		4	00
	1	Dz Idols (match safes)			90
	2	2 large Idols	35		70
large	7	pcs. San Ildefonso (Red)	30	2	10
	3	" Cochiti (light)	25		75
	1	Canteen & belt			75
	3	Blk pitchers	15		45
	3	" pcs small	10		30
	4	" red plain	15		60
	2	" " "	10		20
	3	Bottles Grey plain	10		30
	1	Mexican mug			25
		Indian Blue bread & corn			10

* Established 1861.

Santa Fe, N. M., 189__

M __

In Account with GOLD'S FREE MUSEUM AND OLD Q'ROSITY SHOP.

Wholesale and Retail Dealer in

Indian and Mexican Pottery, Navajo Blankets,

Apache Water Baskets, Cactus Plants and Canes, Stone Vessels from the Cliff Dwellers.
Furs, Robes, Rugs, Wax and Feather Work.

Terms   JAKE GOLD, Propr.   San Francisco Street.

	2	pipes	25		50
	3	Indian drills	25		75
	4	war club	35	1	40
				$14	05

By Wells-Fargo Express to
Mr. E. P. Ripley,
Great Northern Building
Chicago.
Received payment.

Jake Gold

Invoice from well-known early Santa Fe trader, dated 1898. Notice on line one that pottery was often sold in large lots for very low prices. The San Ildefonso pottery on line four could well be worth $1200.00 each today. Photograph by Cradoc Bagshaw.

. . . because of their innate traditional conservatism, Pueblo potters evolved a succession of styles that were remarkably independent of outside influence until the coming of the railroads about 1880, when wider markets provided a commercial stimulus for many of the pueblos.[8]

The more brightly colored Black-on-red pottery, and especially the Polychrome wares, had more appeal to the non-Indian buyer, and quickly replaced the older Black-on-cream ware. Some traditional forms continued, particularly for domestic use, but the tourists encouraged smaller pieces and new non-Indian forms such as pitchers, vases, and candlesticks.

The railroad also brought modern kitchenware containers in more abundant supply. Even more than before, these manufactured wares replaced native pottery in the Pueblo household. There was some sale of better and larger vessels to shops in Santa Fe, but this was limited. Often a trader would buy pottery by the wagon load, selecting the best pieces and destroying the remainder. The newly developed tourist trade did not encourage potters to their best full-sized work, since travelers wanted small pieces.

By 1900 there was again a slump in pottery-making, and only a few potters continued to work.[9] By 1907 the degeneration of San Ildefonso pottery was almost complete.[10] Black-on-red ware was not as well polished, and the paint was improperly prepared and aged. Polychrome ware declined in technical and artistic excellence. In addition, many non-Indian vessel shapes were introduced. By 1907 the potter's art was in a bad way.[11]

Certificate of Baptism

✝

Holy Cross Church

Santa Cruz, New Mexico

This is to Certify

That _Maria Antonia Montoya_

Child of _Tomas Montoya_

and _Reyes Pena_

born in _San Ildefonso, N. Mex._

on the _5_ day of _April_ 1887.

was

Baptized

on the _10_ day of _April_ 1887.

According to the Rite of the Roman Catholic Church

by the Rev. _C. Seux._

the Sponsors being { _Antonio Medina_ _Justa Marina_

as appears from the Baptismal Register of this Church.

Dated _Decbr - 22 - 1952._

Rev. Salvador Genz, P.Y.

Pastor

Maria Antonia Montoya: Certificate of Baptism. Photograph by Cradoc Bagshaw.

CHAPTER THREE

Maria and Julian

*T*HE STORY OF POTTERY REVIVAL at San Ildefonso is the story of Maria and Julian Martinez. In fact, the example of their success was so evident to other potters that it became a strong influence at neighboring pueblos in the revival of their own pottery traditions.

In 1907 the newly founded School of American Research, under the direction of Dr. Edgar L. Hewett, began excavations of prehistoric Pueblo sites on the Pajarito Plateau. Local Indian men were hired as diggers, Maria's husband, Julian Martinez, among them. During the 1908 excavations, Maria was at the camp and saw the pottery sherds that had been uncovered by the diggers. She showed great interest in these ancient decorated pottery fragments and was encouraged by Dr. Hewett to try to reproduce, as nearly as she could, the decorated Polychrome (not black) pottery of the prehistoric inhabitants. This project excited her, and after careful study and preparation, she and Julian were able to produce some vessels by the time Dr. Hewett returned for the next season. They were not merely reproductions of the ancient ware but were exciting art forms in their own right. Dr. Hewett immediately purchased the pieces, and orders were placed for more. As Maria relates, "It was Dr. Hewett that gave me my first interest in pottery." Thus began the now legendary story of Maria,* the potter of San Ildefonso.

---

*The date of Maria's birth is not certain, since there was no record made at the time. Alice Marriott gives 1881 as the year, but states that there is no positive record (Marriott, p. xix). Chapman, whose research is well respected, gives 1887 (Chapman, *The Pottery of San Ildefonso Pueblo*, p. 25). Popovi Da researched the date of his mother's birth in 1952, in order to have a Certificate of Baptism made, and also arrived at the year 1887. If 1887 is correlated with events in Maria's life, such as her marriage in 1904, it seems to work well. In 1904 Maria would have been seventeen years old (based on the 1887 birthdate), which would be a typical age for a young Pueblo woman of that period to be married. It can be safely stated that she was born no later than 1887 and that that date is probably accurate.

Figure 3.1 *Left,* San Ildefonso Polychrome water jar (c. 1890), 9¼″ x 11½″. Unsigned (On October 20, 1974, Maria Martinez and Desideria Sanchez inspected this pot and both agreed that it was made by Nicolasa Peña Montoya. They also believed that the decoration was painted by either her husband or her son.) Courtesy Mr. and Mrs. Grant Wilkins, Colorado. Photograph by Robert Nugent.

Maria first attempted pottery-making as a child of about seven or eight, fashioning dishes for play. She had the advantage of being able to watch two excellent potters then working in the classical San Ildefonso tradition. One was Martina Montoya, who even today remains one of the greatest San Ildefonso potters of all time. Working with her

Figure 3.1 *Right*, Melon jar, polished red with tan underbody (c. 1905), 10½″ x 12½″. Unsigned (attributed to Nicolasa Peña Montoya). Courtesy School of American Research, Indian Arts Fund, Catalog Number IAF 1370. Photograph by Laura Gilpin.

husband, Florentino, who painted the designs on their Polychrome vessels in a most artistic and skillful fashion, they continued to produce outstanding San Ildefonso pottery until they moved to Cochiti Pueblo between 1902 and 1905.

A more important influence was Nicolasa Peña Montoya, Maria's aunt. An excellent potter (Figure 3.1), it was she who encouraged and taught the young Maria in spite of her mother's protestations of "Don't go and bother your aunt." Maria maintained this interest in pottery-making; by the time she was commissioned by Dr. Hewett to make the special pieces, she had acquired the necessary skills and knowledge to make small pieces and successfully complete the task.

17

(Text continues on page 30)

When I got married, then one of my uncles said, "Why you want to marry that boy? He's just a fisherman, fishing in the river; killing bird, or catching bird. He's no farmer. He doesn't know anything about farm. He doesn't know any work or anything. I don't know why you want to marry him." And I didn't say anything. But when he asked me again, I say, "I love him." And that's the way it happened.

My father passed away and he left a whole bunch of cows, everything; turkeys, chickens, farm; and that's the truth that he said that he doesn't know anything. He just go and work in Colorado and no farm, no cows, no nothing.

Julian's father made sifters, those that they sift the flour, made with horsehair. And he sell those to the Indians.

And my husband, I didn't see him work on that sifter. Not even farm. But I married him. And then afterwards, when he was a good-size man, they go to work at Colorado, where the railroad was.

Afterward we tell him that sister Anna, everybody bother her to put design [on pottery], and her husband, he was a painter, Anna's husband. He could paint design, and people, dances on paper. He was an artist, I think the first artist, Crescencio Martinez. And then Julian tried to paint. He paint one and then he hide it. And that's the way he learned to paint the pottery. After a while he was very good.

And when Dr. Hewett came, he bought those pots, and Julian put the designs. There's where we start making a little money, and we were very happy, because we get for one of those seventy-five cents, big jars, or a dollar and a quarter. And we were oh, very happy!

[In this photograph] he was just finished dancing the Eagle Dance, Julian. You see he still has the paint. And this is Adam. That was in St. Louis, I think [1904].

MARIA

18

Maria and Julian and son Adam. St. Louis, 1904.

Julian painting with a yucca brush (c. 1940).

Julian was a good man, and he was head of some ceremony, and he became governor. Sometimes they re-elect him to take care of his people. And at a ceremony, in Indian way, he was very good.

He helped me. He helped me with everything. And I wasn't good myself. I wasn't good. I guess no people — all the time ask Mother Earth to help me and keep me well. [She felt she wasn't the best person and so asked Mother Earth to help her.]

And then he learned artist, and put design on pottery, and fire. Po learned the same. Po and me, sometime I have something to do, well, Po fires my pottery.

Oh, we had a nice life. I never had any trouble with anybody. Specially when Julian was governor, we had to take care of the people. And help the poor, and help every little thing they do. But Julian was a good man, too. He was never like other men; he was not selfish. My sons, too. They don't say to me, 'Don't give or don't do that,' no. They listen to me. So we had a nice life, I think.

I wish I had a girl, I said, so I teach the pottery.

I'm happy. And I say, the Mother Earth will help, and then teach their children that are coming.

I was always happy. I don't send him [Julian] to go and work and earn this and that, no. I do it myself.

We were working together.

And then they carved them. And that carving Julian started too. But it was hard to polish. Sometimes a little piece chipped off and Julian didn't like it. And he said, "Oh, I better paint than to carve." So he paint.

MARIA

Me and my sister just started, nobody else. No, no one didn't say, "make pottery." I myself start on little pots, and my mother used to say, "Don't go over and bother your aunt; you just make little things here."

"But I want to learn."

"Well, you can learn when you grow up a lady."

I was just young, maybe, I don't know how old, maybe thirteen or twelve . . . but we used to sit and watch her. And my mother used to say, "Don't go and bother your aunt."

My Aunt Nicolasa. And she used to make those water [jars], to carry water, and to mix the dough, and to wash the hair.

That's what I say to my mother, "Next time if the aunt give me a clay, then I'm going to try it out."

"No, no, no," my mother said. "Don't bother her. If you want to learn that, go ahead and learn slowly, you learn it slowly without bothering anybody. Just go ahead and watch her how she mix the clay, and then you can make it yourself. And don't bother your aunt." That's what my mother used to say.

I just learned it for myself. I learn it with my, I think my whole heart.

I learned before my sister did, before Anna. And when I married in 1904, I went to St. Louis World's Fair. We were married in the morning and at three o'clock we went in a train. And there I made little pots.

And then she make cheese, my mother, queso. *So I sell it for a dime, and she got a little basket and put in the cheese, and then I bring it down to the pueblo and go in the houses selling cheese. And the ladies called me* quesa *[cheese girl].*

My mother used to say, "Don't go and bother those pottery-makers" [Martina Montoya and Nicolasa Peña]. And I said, "Why? They were nice, and they told me I could watch them." Specially my Aunt Nicolasa. But in those days they just make [pottery to be used] to eat, and to drink atole, *and to mix chili or soup, or dough for bread; all those kinds they used to make; to wash our hair. And I said to my children, "I used to remember after the rain passed that those big, great big olla, they were outside where they collect the rain."*

First we made the cooking pots, usually, and I was the one that made those water jars, but in the black . . . We mostly made it for our own use, for we wash clothes, and we wash our heads, and then the cooking pots.

Those days nobody buy pottery. [We] just sell it [at] Santa Clara or San Juan for wheat, or corn, or chile. But no money.

But my mother didn't see me when I'm learning how to make pottery. She went away in 1909, my mother. I was still young. And my father went in 1914. Julian died in 1943.

22

And my sister used to paint; Anna, the oldest. But when the men are working on the fields, then my sister paint my pottery, too. And sometimes I make bowls for my sister, because she help me paint my pots. And we both worked together, Anna and me. And then later Juanita, Desideria . . . we all make at the same time. We all make the same amount.

I fired them [referring to her sister's pottery]. The black I fire for them, but not those [Polychrome]. Anna fired the Polychrome. I fire my Polychrome myself. I do my own.

Isabel, she's my cousin. I learned from her mother, Nicolasa. And Nicolasa's husband put the design, too, on her pots. Nicolasa didn't paint. But her husband, he's the one, Juan Cruz Montoya, Nicolasa's husband. And her son, Alfredo Montoya, he paint too. He paint pottery. But mostly animals and flowers, like that. And he paint watercolor, too. One time I saw a pot that Alfredo paint when he was in school. He paint the American flag. Alfredo, that is Nicolasa's older son.

Crescencio and Anna [painted my pottery]. And Julian . . . sometimes Arsenio [Sanchez]. Anna was very good, but not so good as Julian and Santana and Crescencio.

And that Awa Tsireh paint his mother's pottery.

But this Florentino [husband of Martina Montoya], he was old, and he painted, oh, very good. But that time I didn't make any pottery, in those days.

Po was getting very good, too. [Is Julian better] than Po? Yeah, sure, he's better than Po. But Po was getting good, too. Now I can look one that Po paints and one Julian, and I can't tell it.

And when Crescencio paint, too, just the same; Julian and Crescencio.

But Alfredo we know his painting by the flowers and the birds, and things like that.

But long time the man didn't make pottery. But now they begin to make pottery. Long time they paint and — they paint figures with watercolor [watercolor paintings]. I know the first one was Crescencio Martinez. And then later Julian, and then later Romando [Vigil] and Awa Tsireh, and now that Desi [J. D. Roybal]* and Gilbert Atencio.

The old man [Julian] paints the same as Po. There's no difference; but that's my pottery. I can tell my pottery by the feel of inside. It's smooth. I will recall it right away. . . . Every lady make different, you see. Not the same. But my sister [Maximiliana] and me we make a little the same, but I can still tell my pots.

---

*J. D. Roybal died on June 28, 1978.

23

Julian digging clay. Courtesy New Mexico State Tourist Bureau. Photograph by Wyatt Davis.

Maria coiling a pot. Courtesy Museum of New Mexico. Photograph by Wyatt Davis.

Shaping the vessel with a gourd.

Applying the wet clay slip to the bowl.

Polishing damp slip with a polishing stone.

24

But this [clay] is harder to [get] — now we get it easy. Just get it. [This one] is more plastic, and the other clay is a little too sandy. [This one's] just like Santa Clara. They have good clay. Acoma and Santa Clara, they can sure make things.

Julian outlining the design on the bowl.
Photograph courtesy New Mexico State
Tourist Bureau.

Maria tending the fire.

Sometimes the good potters leave a little lump in the pottery. And I don't. I smooth it, everything. And I was the one that start the sandpaper. And before that time we just scraped and then rubbed it . . . I start the sandpaper. I learn it from the Museum. I watch them. They make those chairs and tables, and they smooth them with sandpaper. And when I come home I smooth my pottery with sandpaper. There is where I got that sandpaper business. And Julian used to help me. And I said to him, "Don't you get that coarse sandpaper. Get the fine kind." Then I smooth it [the pottery] with water and then put the paint [slip]. And so they come bright, pretty.

They still have the old ones, the first one that I start, at the museum in Santa Fe.

That guaco, we had to boil it, oh, like syrup. We have to cook, cook, cook, long time. And some young people, they don't cook enough. (Some young ones cook it fast, before the spinach get relieved of its hotness, and it doesn't stick.) And then we sift it, sift it in a screen; and then take it outside and put it in a flat bowl, and it dries like candy. And after it dries, then we take it out and break it and store it. Every time

25

Maria and Julian firing pottery.
Courtesy Museum of New Mexico.

Julian removing pottery from the firing pit.
Courtesy Museum of New Mexico.

we want to use it we get a piece and then soak it in water, and then we have to work, work, work it. Then they paint the polychrome.

And some, they don't boil enough, so sometimes it paints a little clear, with little lines. We have to have patience for everything.

But we had to keep the guaco for two, three years. Then it would be good; then it would be strong.

That's the way it looks, my place. Lots of pottery, all kinds, all kinds of shapes. And we had people every day, but sell the pottery cheap.

When people come, this size [ten-inch bowl], I sell them for a dollar. And maybe this large one [water jar], maybe two dollars. Those plates [fourteen inches] were a dollar and a quarter. And now I'm sad about the price [being so high].

And that time the pottery isn't worth anything. And I said to myself, "When I make pottery maybe I would help old people." That's my idea all the time. I'm not a dress woman, fix up myself; and I work, work, and then help people; all my life. And my mother was the same. My father, he was a cowboy and a farmer and he built houses. We all worked, my father, my mother. They were all busy, busy people.

This is pretty, fifteen-inch plate. I sold it for twelve dollars. And I was happy. I was glad, very glad.

And this little feather here [in her hair], roadrunner. I belonged to the ceremony [society]. [Maria has been head of an important women's ceremonial society since 1909.]

Maria with some of her outstanding work. Photograph by Tyler Dingee.

The Sisters: Clara, Desideria, Maria, Maxmiliana (Anna), and Juanita.

And I had my sister that came next to me [Desideria]. She doesn't like to take picture [have her picture taken]. And she's younger than me and her hands get that . . . rheumatism. And she doesn't make pottery, [but] she used to. And the old one was Anna. Anna and then me, and then Desideria, and then Juanita, and then Clara. We just had one brother, but he passed away.

Here we are, young and . . . How we cut our hair! Straight . . . ooh! And we both had long hair, about here [down to her knees]. All the sisters. Just Clara, she doesn't have long hair. But four of us had long [hair] . . . I had a picture, I thought I gave it to Carmelita [Dunlap], but now I don't know who took it, when there was Anna and Carmelita's mother [Juanita]; [it] was taken in Frijole after they finished washing their hair. Oh, pretty!

This is me again, polishing. Now Clara, you should see how she polish. Clara does all the polishing for Santana now. Santana isn't doing any polishing any more, including all the big ones, too. Clara I teach.

And you see how I used to polish. Oh, very nice! Nobody used to polish like me.

But I was the only one that work nearly every day. Those others, they just work — they start in June, July, August, and then when that chile harvest, corn harvest come, then they quit. And the other ladies, they didn't care, poor things. They just make pottery for the 4th of July, and after that they had to work on gardens.

28

Maria smoothing pottery with a gourd.

Maria applying the clay slip.

Maria polishing with a stone.

Maria and Clara polishing.

Photographs on this page by Laura Gilpin.

At this time Julian first worked with the yucca brush* and painted designs on Maria's vessels. Having a natural artistic aptitude, he quickly achieved proficiency, painting the decoration for the first commissioned pieces. He had already acquired skills as a painter, having been encouraged by Dr. Hewett, who supplied him with paper and paints, to draw dance figures.

Before Julian became Maria's partner in pottery-manufacturing, her pottery had been decorated by her sister, Maximiliana (Anna), and by Maximiliana's husband Crescencio Martinez. These, of course, were early unsigned pieces. With the exception of a very few experimental pieces, Maria never decorated pottery herself.

Julian rapidly became the leading pottery decorator at San Ildefonso. His work was characterized by the abundant use of narrow lines and designs composed of many intricate elements which were impressive for the amount of detailed and careful work lavished upon them.

Being a perfectionist and innovator, he was always searching for new ideas in technique and design. Having worked with the archaeologists at various sites, and at the Museum of New Mexico, he compiled a notebook of designs which appealed to him. This notebook was burned, according to the Pueblo tradition of burning personal possessions, upon his death in 1943. He gathered material from various prehistoric as well as historic† sources. His adaptation of the prehistoric Mimbres feather design is well known and now widely used by Pueblo potters (Figure 3.4). He is also credited with reviving nineteenth century San Ildefonso Black-on-cream pottery designs (Figures 3.5 and 3.6) and the adaptation of the Pueblo *avanyu* (water serpent or plumed serpent) (Figure 3.12). This design element is now used by all San Ildefonso potters and has even become popular with neighboring Pueblo potters, especially at Santa Clara. Julian was also impressed by the Hopi potter Nampeyo. Her influence in some of his work is evident, particularly during the 1920s.

Bunzel states that Julian influenced San Ildefonso decorative style more than any other person and felt that his designs, which were

> . . . executed with such exquisite technical perfection, and such an unerring sense of the limitations and possibilities of his technique . . . were incomparably freer than anything else produced in San Ildefonso, or, indeed, in the whole Southwest.[1]

---

*The use of the yucca brush is as old as the earliest decorated prehistoric southwestern pottery.

†The generally accepted date for dividing prehistoric from historic pottery is about A.D. 1600. In other words, written history began with the advent of the Spanish in New Mexico, so that pottery made after that time is termed historic.

Concerning the pottery revival at San Ildefonso, she also writes:

> The leaders of this movement were Maria Martinez and more especially her husband Julian, who decorated all of Maria's pottery. He is a skillful painter, and a man of considerable originality and sensitiveness to problems of design . . . He was a discriminating student and a receptive one . . .[2]

With the encouragement of Dr. Hewett and Kenneth Chapman of the School of American Research, Maria and Julian developed rapidly in the ceramic arts. As interest in Pueblo pottery increased, other potters, too, began improving their work.

> It was suggested to some who were known to be good potters, that they attempt to revive their art, to try to emulate the excellence of the ancient wares. While the response was not immediate, there was observable, during the next few years, a distinct improvement in the pottery of San Ildefonso. Realizing the importance of this, the authorities of the Museum of New Mexico and the School of American Research threw themselves heartily into the task of stimulating the industry. They urged the women to do better and better work, and in particular induced them to return to the sound canons of native art . . .
>
> The undertaking was not an easy one, however, for it was difficult to get most of the women to go to the trouble of making good pieces when the tourists, who were still the principal purchasers, were equally or even better pleased with imitations of china water pitchers . . . and candlesticks. The problem thus resolved itself into one of supplying a market. The Museum bought many good pieces, and Mr. Chapman, who from the beginning had been a leading spirit in the attempt at rehabilitating the art, himself purchased large amounts of pottery, never refusing a creditable piece, never accepting a bad one.
>
> Progress was slow, but eventually certain women, becoming interested in their work, made real progress both technically and artistically. Their products began to sell more freely and at better prices than did those of others. Antonita Roybal, Ramona Gonzales, Maximiliana Martinez, and Maria Martinez all turned out fine vessels, the two latter being greatly aided by their husbands, who developed into skillful decorators. Maria especially shone. By 1915 she had far surpassed all the others, her pots were in great demand, and at the present time [1925] she has a ready market, at prices which ten years ago would have seemed fantastic, for everything she can find time to make.
>
> From the point of view of ceramics the development has been most interesting. Maria began with the manufacture of

Figure 3.2   Polychrome jar, Cochiti slip (1926); made by Maria Martinez in 1926; purchased from Maria and accessioned by the Indian Arts Fund in 1928; price tag on bottom of pot: $22.00; 15½″ x 19″. Signature: Marie, San Ildefonso N.M. Courtesy School of American Research, Indian Arts Fund, Catalog Number IAF 1166. Photograph by Jerry Jacka.

Figure 3.3   Side view of Polychrome jar in Figure 3.2. Photograph by Jerry Jacka.

polychrome ware, as that was the style most commonly being made at the time. The shapes were improved, the finish of the surfaces was given greater attention, and the decorations were applied with a surer, more delicate touch. Black-on-red ware [Figure 3.10] was taken in hand, the old-time polish was restored, the vegetable paint properly prepared and aged. Polished black was also reintroduced [Figure 6.19]; pieces of this sort, with their simple, graceful shapes and high black gloss sold so well that they soon became an important product.[3]

Maria usually handled the Cochiti slip on the Polychrome wares well and avoided the grey, grainy, and streaked surfaces that characterized the finish of other potters. Maria's revival of polished Black ware, more highly polished than ever before, was an immediate success (Figure 6.19).

Beginning in 1911, Maria and Julian, along with other potters, were allowed to demonstrate their craft at the Museum of New Mexico in Santa Fe, and to sell directly to the public, which furthered superior form and surface finish. Kenneth Chapman encouraged Maria and Julian to use native designs in the decoration of their pottery, which also helped to spark a revival of excellence in the making of Indian pottery.

By 1915 Maria had mastered the art of making larger vessels and had attained a skill that surpassed all other San Ildefonso potters. Her pottery was characterized by relatively thin walls, hard firing, careful forming, smooth and clear finishes, carefully applied and well-executed designs, and in the case of Black ware, a highly lustrous surface polish.

> The degree of polish obtained by different potters varies considerably . . . Maria Martinez, who does the best polishing, is also the swiftest worker in the village. From the moment the vessel is picked up to apply the slip until the completion of the polishing, it is not laid down for an instant. Her strokes are quicker than those of the other potters; she covers the surface in much less time and therefore polishes a given area more often before the slip dries.[4]

She was acknowledged by all informed observers as the master potter of San Ildefonso. Her friends and relatives, seeing her success, began to attempt to improve their own wares by copying her techniques.

During World War I tourist travel in New Mexico decreased and Pueblo pottery sales fell off. Other potters had not achieved Maria's and Julian's technical perfection and artistic excellence. There was still need to encourage other potters to do their best work. It was during this period that Mme. Verra von Blumenthal, who had successfully revived lace-making in Russia, and Miss Rose Dougan of Pasadena tried to encourage the development of pottery so high in quality that demand for it

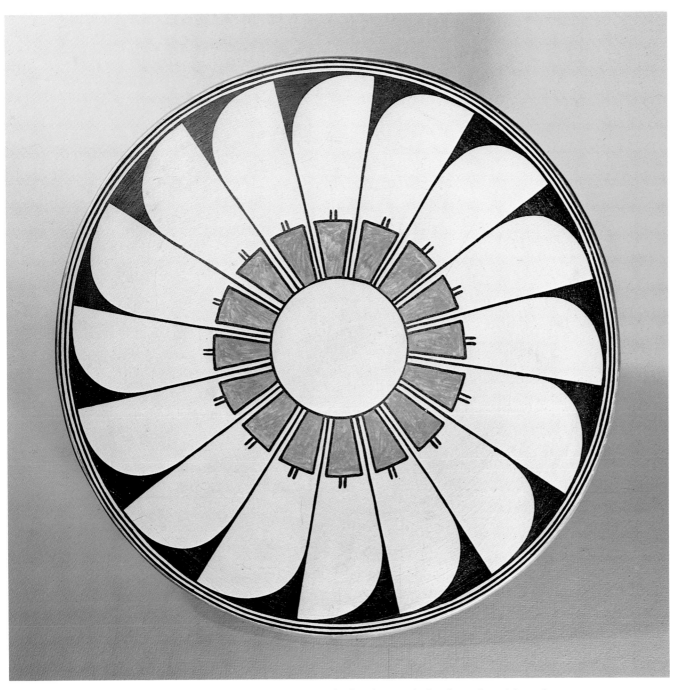

Figure 3.4   Polychrome plate (c. 1925); a wide feather design which Julian adapted from the earlier Mimbres style; in later years Julian made the feather increasingly narrower; 12″ diameter. Signature: Marie. Courtesy Mr. and Mrs. Dennis Lyon, Scottsdale. Photograph by Jerry Jacka.

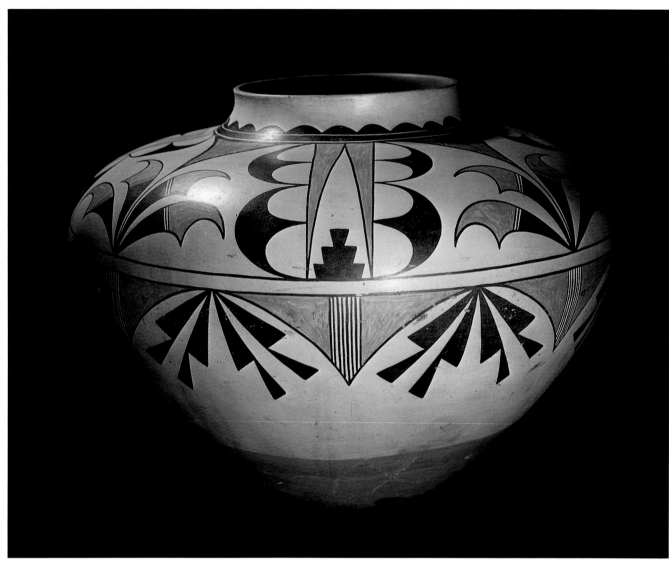

Figure 3.5   Polychrome storage jar, Cochiti slip (c. 1925); large Polychrome ware incorporating plant forms in the design, 15″ x 20½″. Signature: Eroded with definite evidence of Marie ("ie" shows), possible evidence of Julian. Courtesy Museum of New Mexico, Catalog Number 18780/12. Photograph by Jerry Jacka.

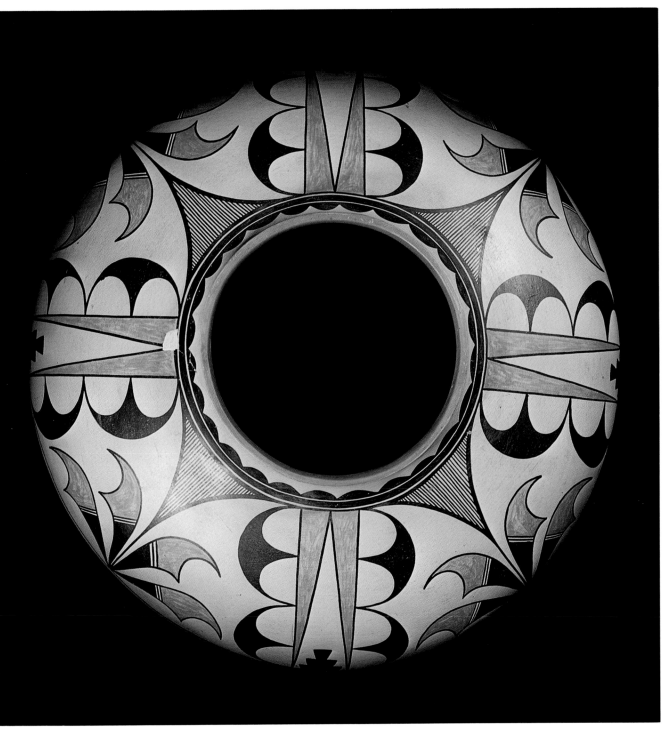

Figure 3.6   Top view of Polychrome storage jar in Figure 3.5. Photograph by Jerry Jacka.

Figure 3.7   Polychrome jar, Cochiti slip (c. 1925); use of kachina sun faces, sun rays, *avanyu* and modified feather motifs, 9¾" x 13¼". Signed: Marie. This is an example of Julian's painting at its finest. Private Collection. Photograph by Jerry Jacka.

would be nationwide. However, they only spent the summer months working with this project; by the end of the summer of 1919 it became obvious that little had been accomplished. As a result, they turned the project over to the Museum of New Mexico, headed by Dr. Hewett, giving an annual subsidy of $200. Kenneth Chapman and Wesley Bradfield directed the experiment to convince the potters that better quality pottery, although taking more time, was worth the effort because of the higher price it would bring.

> [During the winter of 1920] Julian and Maria Martinez of San Ildefonso appeared with a wagon load of their pottery. Here was an unexpected problem. They were the last we would have picked for our experiment, for they were accomplished craft workers who might resent our suggestions for improvement of their wares. However, we knew that they were forced to limit the time expended on each piece, for they had learned that the dealers would not pay higher prices for a more finished product. So, in hopes in finding one or more outstanding pieces in the lot, we decided to test our plan. It worked wonders! We set aside four unusually well formed and finished pieces and asked their prices. Then we commended the couple for the attractive qualities of their pottery and paid twenty-five percent more than they had asked. That concluded, we told them of our plan and promised even more for others in their next lot if they showed further improvement.[5]

By 1919 Maria and Julian were producing vessels that were not only technically outstanding, but artistically superior. The classical shapes were flawless and the new shapes were well-proportioned, graceful, and pleasing. Julian's sense of design worked in harmony with the surface he was to decorate, creating masterpieces in pottery art.

It was in 1919 that experiments begun by Maria and Julian resulted in the now famous matte-black-on-polished-black ware (Figures 3.11–3.15). Different authors have given different dates for this discovery: Chapman, 1919; Guthe, 1921; Goddard, 1921; Toulouse, 1919; Bunzel, 1921; and Marriott, 1919. Marriott has stated:

> The exact date of the invention of black-on-black pottery at San Ildefonso has not been determined. The discovery took place in 1918 or 1919, according to Mrs. Martinez. The first piece of whose sale there is a record was accessioned in 1920 by the Museum of New Mexico.[6] (Figure 3.11).

Figure 3.8   Polychrome jar, Cochiti slip (c. 1929); water jar of the late Polychrome period; designs include feathers, plant forms, clouds, and delicately executed line-work for which Julian was well known, 10¼″ x 12½″. Signature: Marie. Courtesy Mr. and Mrs. Dennis Lyon, Scottsdale. Photograph by Jerry Jacka.

Figure 3.9   Polychrome jar, Cochiti slip (1927); "Snake Pot"; this jar is the best known of Maria's and Julian's Polychrome ware, 11¼" x 12½". Signature: Marie & Julian. Courtesy Da Collection, San Ildefonso. Photograph by Jerry Jacka.

The date of 1919 seems quite certain. Obviously the 1921 date is incorrect. A Black-on-black piece (Figure 3.11) was on display at the Museum of New Mexico during the summer of 1920:

> In the Acoma Alcove at the Keresan Gallery of the New Museum has been placed an exhibit of seventeen of the most artistic pieces of pottery by Marie of San Ildefonso which the Museum has acquired for its collection. Even the casual visitor will recognize that the pieces are extraordinarily handsome and that they represent the highest type and finest development of Pueblo Art. Several highly polished pieces of black ware, in form and luster, are exquisite, while the largest black olla is in dull finish with a plumed serpent in luster winding its sinuous form around the entire vessel, the effect being surprisingly impressive. It is a piece of handicraft and artistic decoration that will stand comparison with the best that has come out of the Orient or the Occident, ancient or modern.[7]

The response to the new ware was not immediate. As previously stated, the first pieces were finished in matte with only the design polished. After further experimentation, this process was changed (compare Figure 3.11 and Figure 3.12) to incorporate the polished design within a band on a polished vessel. The new Black-on-black ware was then much more attractive, and the new process quickly became popular.

> The invention of matte painting on a polished surface by Julian Martinez in 1919 was a true discovery, even though archaeological excavations in southwestern New Mexico during recent years have yielded numerous sherds bearing evidence of similar experiments . . . In 1919 in his first experiments with matte painting on polished wares, Julian chose as the motif his own version of the *avanyu* (plumed serpent), which he had developed through occasional use in Polychrome decoration. With this he had his choice of painting the *avanyu* in solid matte on an unfired, polished vessel, or of producing a polished *avanyu* upon the matte surface of an unpolished vessel.
>
> He chose the latter. He outlined the wavy form of an *avanyu* encircling the moistened body of a jar and then left the polishing to Maria. It was a difficult task. She could not use a free sweeping motion of the polishing stone. This left the edges uneven. Although they could be more sharply defined by retouching the edges of the surrounding matte surface with a brush, the combination was not satisfactory because of the comparatively great expanse of matte surface which was unattractive to the eye and harsh to the touch. The

Figure 3.10   Black-on-red jar (c. 1925); one of the few examples of Black-on-red ware by Maria and Julian; cloud and butterfly designs, possibly Hopi inspired, 8½" x 14½". Signature: Marie. Private Collection. Photograph by Jerry Jacka.

Figure 3.11   Black-on-black jar (1919 or 1920); *avanyu* (water serpent) design with matte background; the first Black-on-black vessel of which there is a record, 8½" x 13", unsigned. Courtesy Museum of New Mexico, Catalog Number 18702/12. Photograph by Jerry Jacka.

44

Figure 3.12   Black-on-black jar (c. 1924); long-necked vase with *avanyu* design, 13½″ x 9″.
Signature: Marie. Private Collection. Photograph by Jerry Jacka.

Figure 3.13 Black-on-black jars. *Left,* Black-on-black jar (1930s) with plant forms and clouds in combination with geometric designs, 9⅜″ x 11″. Signature: Marie & Julian. Courtesy Museum of New Mexico, Catalog Number 25014/12. *Middle,* Black-on-black storage jar (1942); a superb example of Maria's potting skill and Julian's design style using fine lines, plant forms, geometric and stylized bird motifs, 18¾″ x 22″. Signature: Marie & Julian. School of American Research Collections in the Museum of New Mexico, Catalog Number 31595/12. *Right,* Black-on-black jar (1940), 3⅞″ x 5⅞″. Signature: Marie & Julian. Courtesy Museum of New Mexico, Catalog Number 12328/12. Photograph by Jerry Jacka.

Figure 3.14   Top view of center jar in Figure 3.13. Photograph by Jerry Jacka.

47

lack of sales appeal led the couple to abandon their initial experiments. Only a few specimens of this type were made, and rarely has one been preserved. But through further adjustments of the combination of polish and matte, the defects were eventually remedied in 1921 by first outlining with a brush an encircling zone on a well polished jar and then outlining the *avanyu* within it.

The resulting spaces above and below the *avanyu* were then filled with the matte paint, thus producing the effect of a polished *avanyu* within a comparatively narrow background of matte, and leaving the greater part of the vessel with its attractive polished surface. By 1921 the *avanyu* design had also been enhanced by outlining a cloud cluster in each of the matte spaces above the downsweep of the *avanyu's* undulating body and by adding the pairs of finlike appendages below. These served further to reduce the areas of matte surface within the decorated zone. With this combination perfected, the essentials of the *avanyu* arrangement have since been maintained with only a few minor variations in details.*

Meanwhile Julian continued his experiments with other motifs but found no other life forms in his San Ildefonso repertoire as suitable as the *avanyu* for use as polished motifs within a matte background. However, in his adaptation of a feather motif from ancient Mimbres pottery, he made a wise choice in revising the combination of black and white by leaving the feathers in polished black and thus subordinating the minor areas used as a matte background.[8] [Figure 3.15]

By 1921 the process was perfected, and Maria began sharing the secret with other potters. The process for Black-on-black ware was actually a simple one. The design was painted with red clay slip on a polished vessel before firing. The pottery was then smoked black in firing in the same firing process used for plain polished Black ware. "For the best black color, the firing must be cool. In fact, if the firing temperature exceeds 650° C., although the ware is much harder and more durable, the resulting shrinkage of the slip produces a greyish gunmetal surface that is less attractive."[9]

Guthe states that Julian used a hard yellow rock, ground to powder and mixed with guaco, for paint.[10] Chapman states that Julian used a mineral substance ground into a powder for paint.[11] Maria says that neither rocks nor guaco were ever used as paint for Black-on-black ware, just clay. She feels, specifically referring to Guthe's discussion, that he must have been confused by her telling him about the way the Acomas and Zunis painted their pottery.

After being perfected, the new Black-on-black ware proved extraordinarily popular; indeed it became world-famous and was much copied. However, Maria and Julian remained the masters. By 1925 practically

*See Figures 3.17, 6.5, 6.9.

all of the San Ildefonso potters were making this ware. Guthe noted, "Maria, however, still produces by far the finest pieces."[12]

The earliest pieces were globular in shape, but innovations in shape came rapidly (Figure 3.12). Julian quickly adapted his painting techniques to the new forms. The *avanyu* and feather designs were popular, but he also revived the geometric motifs of the nineteenth century Black-on-cream ware. "His discriminating and imaginative use of what came his way has produced a style of rare distinction."[13] "No one else achieves the distinction of Julian at his best."[14]

Two events occurred in the 1920s that further encouraged the production of pottery of higher quality. The first Santa Fe Indian Market was held in 1922 under the direction of the School of American Research, aided by donations from interested local citizens. Called the Indian Fair at that time, this had more far-reaching effects than earlier quality encouragements, since all the Pueblos were included. Native clays, pigments, and traditional methods were required in order to participate in the market. Entrants were limited to members of the Southwestern tribes. In 1932 the Market was taken over by the Southwestern Association on Indian Affairs (then known as the New Mexico Association on Indian Affairs). This same organization continues to conduct the Indian Market today. For years Maria consistently won the Indian Market's top awards.

In 1924 a bridge was built across the Rio Grande near San Ildefonso and the highway was improved. Tourist traffic began to travel to the Pueblo to buy directly from the potters. "So, after a century or more as one of the most isolated Tewa pueblos, San Ildefonso finally came into the limelight as the most progressive arts and crafts center among the Rio Grande Pueblos."[15]

Kidder, writing in 1924, makes an important point: "There are still many expert potters, who turn out fine vessels, even with the knowledge that they are to be sold to the White man."[16] Many critics have stated that the technical and artistic excellence of Indian pottery declined rapidly when it started being made for sale to non-Indians rather than for domestic use. But with a few exceptions, this point of view is false. Fine pottery was being made then, and fine pottery continues to be made today, although in decreasing amounts.

It is interesting to note San Ildefonso pottery prices for 1924. "Prices are conditioned by quality of craftsmanship and the fame of the maker . . . a small bowl of decorated black ware by Maria Martinez brings from three to six dollars. Large and unusual pieces, such as prayer meal bowls, vases, bring up to twelve dollars."[17] Other potters received significantly less for their work. A good estimate of Maria's annual income in that year is something in the area of $2,000.

Figure 3.15   Black-on-black storage jar (1940); turkey, feather, and cloud designs, 18¼″ x 20¼″. Signature: Marie & Julian. Courtesy Museum of New Mexico, Catalog Number 18888/12. Photograph by Jerry Jacka.

And the first big one I made in the black is in the museum in Santa Fe. And that one I sold is to that Henry Dendahl. Henry Dendahl. And he said, "How much, Maria?" And I say, "Oh, you can give me whatever you want." And he gave me forty. I nearly fall down. Forty dollars and three shawls. So I gave one to Adam's wife, and another one to Po's wife, and one I kept. And I and my sister, we polished it, one on one side and the other on the other side. That was Maximiliana. Not Clara. That was Anna.

MARIA

Figure 3.16 Black-on-black jar (1952); feather and kiva-step designs, 9¾″ x 10½″. Signature: Marie & Santana. Collection of author, Santa Fe. Photograph by Jerry Jacka.

Maria molding and Santana painting pottery. Photograph by Harvey Caplin.

Santana is painting. That's what people like, when I [make] the edge straight. And perfect.

[Santana started making pottery] after she married to Adam. She lived seven years with me, so she make pottery. Her mother make pottery; Tonita make pottery, her aunt; and her grandmother, Domingita. She comes from a [family of] good potters, too. But she didn't make any pottery until she was married to Adam. She sure can draw design too.

And Santana, didn't try the red [Black-on-red] or Polychrome; just Black.

And her uncle is Crescencio Martinez, my sister's husband. He painted pottery and he painted [dance] figures, and that's Santana's uncle. Santana's mother and Crescencio and Tonita are brothers and sisters. Santana didn't make any pottery when she was young. But after she married with Adam, then she learned from me. And she paints. [She learned from] Julian. And she's very good at painting.

She really know how to paint; she's doing it herself now. She now polish it herself, but before I used to polish it for her. I am the one that polished this one. It's really nice painting; it's nicely made.

52

The economic importance of pottery-making became increasingly significant. The income from pottery began to exceed the income from farm products. A dramatic rise in the standard of living was evident.

> The government agents in some pueblos state that since the younger women have taken to pottery-making, half of the domestic troubles of the Indians have disappeared, and in the Pueblo of San Ildefonso, for example, new houses with better sanitary conditions and improved comforts and happiness can, in a large degree, be traced to the economic success of the ceramic artists.[18]

By 1931 Maria's annual income was over $5,000. She hired Spanish household help so that she could devote more time to pottery-making. Other Indians, envious of Maria's and Julian's prosperity, became more interested in taking up the dying art. Maria began to hold pottery classes both at San Ildefonso and at the Indian School in Santa Fe. For this, the government paid her one dollar per hour.

After Julian's death in 1943, Maria began working with her daughter-in-law, Santana. Maria did the pottery-making and Santana did the painting (Figures 3.16 and 3.17). Artistically, the Marie and Santana period (1943–1956) is an extension of the late Marie and Julian period, as the same type and style of ware (Black-on-black ware and occasional Red ware continued to be produced although with less emphasis on larger pieces.

Santana comes from an impressive background (See Genealogy, Appendix). Her brother was Awa Tsireh (Alfonso Roybal), considered by many critics to be the most talented of all Pueblo artists. Her mother was Alfonsita Martinez Roybal, an accomplished potter. Her uncle was Crescencio Martinez, one of San Ildefonso's first and most gifted artists and a pottery decorator who was married to Maria's oldest sister, Maximiliana. Her aunt was Tonita Martinez Roybal, generally considered Maria's closest competitor in pottery-making. And her grandmother was Dominguita Pino Martinez, also one of San Ildefonso's better potters, well known for her Black-on-red ware. (Figure 2.2).

After their marriage, Santana and Adam lived with Maria and Julian for eight years, which gave Santana the opportunity to learn both phases of the art from the masters, since she had not worked with pottery before. She continued as Maria's partner until 1956, when Maria began a partnership with her son Popovi Da. At this point, Santana began producing on her own, signing her pieces, "Santana and Adam." Today Santana is considered one of San Ildefonso's leading potters. Her work is characterized by well-formed shapes, careful finishes, and skillful decoration (Figure 3.18).

Figure 3.17 Buff-on-red plate (c. 1947); *avanyu* design, 14″ diameter. Signature: Marie & Santana. Private collection. Photograph by Jerry Jacka.

54

Figure 3.18 Black-on-black jar with lid (c. 1968); feather and kiva-step design, 12¾" x 12¼". Signature: Santana/Adam. Courtesy Mrs. Lorraine Mulberger, Scottsdale. Photograph by Jerry Jacka.

Bow and Arrow Dance at San Ildefonso. The dancers left to right are Viola Martinez, Clara Montoya, Santana Martinez, Angelita Martinez, Anita Martinez, Juanita Roybal, Anna Martinez Montoya, Tomasita Sanchez, Maria Martinez, Isabel Pino, Anita Da, Lupita Roybal Vigil, Isabel Atencio, Santana Vigil Peña Montoya, and an unidentified child. The drummer is Desideria Sanchez. Courtesy Des Art Shop, Santa Fe.

Maria teaching pottery at San Ildefonso. Left to right: Marie Roybal Christian, Esther Vigil, Julian Martinez, Florence Naranjo, Juanita Roybal, Josephine Roybal, Maria Martinez, Tomasita Montoya Sanchez, Clara Montoya, Crucita Gonzales Calabaza (Blue Corn), Tonita Pino Brewer, Lupita Martinez, Felipita Martinez Torres. Photograph by T. Harmon Parkhurst.

I used to teach at the Indian School in Santa Fe, others: students from Domingo, Acoma, Cochiti, San Juan and Santa Clara, the younger people. Oh, they make very good pottery, some of them. I think Santa Clara, they have, oh, very good clay. Acoma and Santa Clara, I like their clay. So I'm glad they are doing fine.

I'm not greedy with my work, so I teach at the government school where Mr. Ferris was superintendent; I teach the other younger people.

56

Maria baking bread. Photograph by Laura Gilpin.

Taking out the bread. Yes, I used to make my bread, every week-end. Because John, my son, was in the school, and he'd bring boys, Zuni boys, Hopi boys to dance at home on Sunday. So I get ready for them. And all these Hopi and the Cochiti, they used to dance at home, [at the] pueblo.

57

San Ildefonso Drummers. Left to right: Atilano Montoya of *The House at Otowi Bridge* fame, Sotero Montoya (Anna's second husband), Donecio Sanchez (Desideria's husband), Miguel Martinez (Anna's son by Crescencio), Encarnación Tafoya, and Domingo.

And I used to have a little cash store, just to support the people. But none of my boys, my sons, they don't like that. They don't want to be bothered with people. So we, after the old man passed away, then we take away the little cash store. Nobody didn't want to bother.

And I took care of my people, and other people. Those that passed away I took care of them, the little old ladies, not only mine. There's some old people that I took care of. After I finished my work I went over and took care of old people when I was young and strong. An old lady I took care. I'm not selfish. I don't hide anything. I give them all they want to eat . . . and I like to help people. I'm not a dressed woman, no. I help people. I help people.

58   *And I have some Spanish . . . and they help me clean the house or wash the clothes, or wash dishes.*

Maria shaping a small pinched pot which is a small pot formed without coil.

And I would say, some Indian ladies they don't like [non-Indian] visitors, and they don't like anyone watching them making pottery. But me, I don't care. Summertime they find me outside making [pottery] . . . I let them see, and if they want they can take picture. After what I think. . . . Big buses come, school buses. I go out and shake hands. Young kids, if they want to take picture, "Oh, let them take." I don't mind. I don't say, "Pay me this and pay me that." No. Sometimes if they want, well, they give me a little, little present, some money. So I'm happy.

This is a small one I made. I made one like this for that Mondale [the Vice-President's wife visited Maria at San Ildefonso on April 18, 1977]. Then she got a nail and I sign it. And I say, "If you don't be careful [it's] going too —" "No, I'm going to take care," she said.
Sometimes I make in California, little one. I don't finish it. Just show them.

59

Maria

on People and Places

HEWETT

He was the one that we know first, and he was the one that start us in pottery. He bought, and then they dug out some old pots, and some of his boys that were there, they say, "Maria, can you make me one like this?" "Sure," I said. So I make them. And then another one come and ask me. From there it came the pottery.

When they dig out [pottery sherds], they take them to my house and ask me if I can make this kind. But the Glaze [ware], I didn't. I didn't make them.

And this Dr. Hewett was the one that put me in interest in pottery. And another one from, his name was Spinden, from New York. And he wears, oh, thick glasses. And the Indians, they call him The Man Who Is Always Looking Down at the Ground. *They said he was the richest man. He just looked and whatever pot he liked he — he'd come to me and I make. And he pay me sometime two dollar, or three dollar for those pots. But we, I was happy.*

But that Dr. Hewett, he was, oh, very good.

But more we learn from Dr. Hewett. And then he take boys from this pueblo to work at the museum, where they start that museum. In the summertime he had a school out of state, I think. So they call us and we go [at the Museum of New Mexico] and we make pottery, and we fire pottery, and there we sell it; come home happy.

CHAPMAN

Yes, Chapman. He used to ask me [a lot of questions] — and I said to Julian, "Let's go home. He asks too many questions." But when we would leave, then sometimes he would give us three dollars. Then we go happy (laughs).

CARL GUTHE

We used to call him Gutie. [Guthe states he watched Maria paint pottery.] Maybe I did when he asked me. Maybe I did, because we saw a picture where I was painting one small one. But maybe he was the one who asked me. But I don't paint.

BLUMENTHAL & DOUGAN

And there was a lady, two ladies. One was old, and the other one was young [Mme. von Blumenthal and Rose Dougan], and they had a ranch out there in the Pajarito Sankawi. And then they would have open house and this lady, everybody know her, she ordered potters to make the pots for her open house. So everybody made pottery, or what they know. And I made a big one. And she say, "We are willing to pay you," and she gave me seven dollars for that big pot.

MAE WEST

And I used to know that Mae, Mae West. Last I met her in Atlanta, Georgia; but she was old. And now she must be very old. And Cornel Wilde, Joseph Cotton, Linda Darnell. And I visit their place in Hollywood. And they took me where their hands and feet are [Grauman's Chinese Theater — 1939].

GERMANY

A man came from Germany to take a picture of my hands. Germany. He came to take a picture of me. And I was telling him why he want picture taken of me. He said because too many people know you and you've been making pottery. I don't know why he want picture of [only] my hands.

Figure 4.1   Water jar with Polychrome body, Black-on-red neck, Cochiti slip (c. 1918); an unusual combination of two types: Black-on-red ware (upper body) and Polychrome ware (lower body) which includes cloud and sun designs, 8¼″ x 10¾″. Signature: Poh've'ha. Courtesy Museum of New Mexico, Catalog Number 18798/12. Photograph by Cradoc Bagshaw.

At that time we didn't know anything about name, how to spell it. And I made Po've'ha. It wasn't the right way to spell it. [c. 1918]

MARIA

CHAPTER FOUR

Signatures

IN THE COURSE OF HER LONG POTTERY CAREER, Maria Martinez has used seven different signatures: Poh've'ka, Marie, Marie & Julian, Marie & Santana, Maria & Santana, Maria Poveka, and Maria/Popovi. These hallmarks have been a matter of much confusion to many people. We hope to clarify the matter here.

The fact that one of the above signatures appears on a piece of pottery does not necessarily mean that it is an authentic piece of Maria pottery. Unfortunately, there have been some forgeries, and in some cases the signature looks quite convincing. On the other hand, there are vessels signed with an "irregular" signature that are definitely Maria's, as will be explained later in this chapter. As of this date, the only legitimate signatures that are foolproof are the fired-in signatures of Maria/Popovi (Figure 4.2) followed by a number (such as "Maria/Popovi 869") and "Maria Poveka" followed by a number (Figure 4.3). These numbers refer to the month and year of firing; for example, 869 is August 1969.

To further confuse the issue, Maria's early pieces were unsigned. As a result, Maria, being a kindly person and not wanting to disappoint anyone by telling them they did not have a Maria pot, has signed her name with a felt pen to many turn-of-the-century San Ildefonso Polychromes. Most of these pots, in fact, are not hers. There are also pieces of Black ware with a signature scratched-in after firing that are not her work. There is even a well-known case of a Santa Clara Black ware vessel with a scratched-in Maria signature and a published photograph of Maria holding this same piece. To Maria's credit, it must be stated that when she realizes that a person honestly wants to know the maker of a pot and that he is not just hoping it will be hers, she seriously attempts to determine the authenticity of the piece.

Maria was the first Pueblo Indian potter to begin the use of her sig-

Figure 4.2 Maria/Popovi 869. Photograph by Jerry Jacka.   Figure 4.3 Maria Poveka 467. Photograph by Jerry Jacka.

nature on her pottery as a regular practice. As she became better known, there was a growing demand for her work, and her signature was used to identify her pieces. 1923 is the generally accepted date when Maria began to sign her pottery. This date is correct with a few exceptions. These exceptions are several pieces finished about 1918 and signed "Poh've'ka" (incorrectly spelled, "Poh've'ha"). Poveka is Maria's Indian name, which translates in English to Pond Lily. There are records of four vessels signed in such a manner.

In the collection of the American Museum of Natural History (Catalogue Number 50.2/1532) is a round plaque or flat tile of 7-9/16 inches diameter, with the signature "Poh've'ka" incised on the back. Marriott (p. 285, illustrated p. 137) dates this piece c. 1925, but according to the records of the American Museum of Natural History, it was purchased from the Museum of New Mexico in 1918.[1]

There is also a record of a second piece from the collection of the American Museum of Natural History in the notes of Richard M. Howard, well-known collector and authority on Pueblo Indian pottery. This is a Black-on-red closed bowl, 9½ inches high by 18 inches in diameter, with a painted signature "Poh've'ka" (Catalogue Number 50.2/1528). This piece is also dated 1918.

A third piece belongs to the Museum of New Mexico (Catalogue Number 12345/12) and is a Polychrome bowl with the signature "Poh've'ka" painted on the interior. This piece is dated 1910–1920.[2]

64

Figure 4.4   Marie. Photograph by Jerry Jacka.

The fourth piece is also in the collection of the Museum of New Mexico (Catalogue Number 18798/12) and is an unusual double-shouldered water jar with a Polychrome body and a neck in Black-on-red, which includes the painted signature, "Poh've'ha" (Figure 4.1). This piece is tentatively dated 1918 also.[3]

Thus, there are at least four examples of signed Maria pottery before the generally accepted date of 1923. However, it was in 1923 that Maria began signing her pottery with the signature "Marie" (Figure 4.4). "Marie" was selected instead of "Maria" because it was suggested that "Marie" was a name more familiar to the non-Indian public.

By 1925 the custom of signing pottery was becoming well established. It was about this time that Julian's name was added to the signature, since he did all of the painting of decoration (Figure 4.5) and helped with firing. The additional signature was probably suggested by Chapman. "Jars signed 'Marie' were collected in 1923; unsigned jars date from as late as 1926. The 'Marie & Julian' signature first appeared about 1925."[4] Popovi Da has stated that the first "Marie and Julian" signature was begun in 1934,[5] but the date 1925 seems fairly certain. It can safely be stated that by 1926 most of the pieces were being signed.

There has been criticism, particularly of the Marie and Marie-and-Julian periods, that Maria did not do all of the work herself. In the period before Julian's name was added to the signature, Bunzel was particularly critical that Maria took all of the credit:

> At San Ildefonso individualism has in some ways reached its highest development. All the more expert potters are known by name to traders and collectors in Santa Fe and elsewhere. A number of them, in fact, are so well-known that they sign their names to all their products. The name is frequently misleading. By no means all of the pottery that goes under Maria Martinez' name is hers. Much of it she has modelled; some of

Figure 4.5 Marie & Julian. Photograph by Jerry Jacka. Figure 4.6 Marie & Julian. Photograph by Cradoc Bagshaw.

it is modelled by her two sisters, and practically all of it is
painted by her husband, Julian. However, the work turned out
by this family is all of surpassing excellence . . . Julian's designs are, on the whole, simpler than Juan's [Juan Cruz Roy-
bal]. Some, which are the last word in brevity of expression,
are unmistakable . . . No other women besides Maria and
Tonita [Roybal] seem to achieve the deep luster of polished jet
which characterizes the finish of bowls of their workmanship.
. . . No one else achieves the distinction of Julian at his best.[6]

In a later study, Whitman adds further criticism:

Maria's skill as a potter and her originality in creating forms
is reflected not only in her pottery but in her relation to the
pottery industry. She turned the front room of her house into
a store where she and her husband sell their pottery, and
where Julian sells his paintings to the tourists arriving in
buses. Realizing that she can command better prices from the
tourists than from traders who sell to them, Maria does not
trade. But she has gone further than this; her unmarried sister
and her daughter-in-law assist her in pottery-making, while
her husband and son help with the decorating. To these pots
she puts her own name and that of Julian. She will also occasionally buy pottery in the village, finish it, and sell it under
her own name.[7]

Most of this criticism is too harsh. First, one must remember that
the signing of pottery was a foreign idea, the significance of which was

Figure 4.7   Marie & Santana. Photograph by Cradoc Bagshaw.   Figure 4.8   Maria/Popovi. Photograph by Jerry Jacka.

probably not totally understood by the traditional Indian potters. To them if the pottery was San Ildefonso, what difference did it make who made it? Also, one must consider that pottery-making was traditionally and often a group or communal affair, with several women working together on various stages of pottery-making. Of course, Maria had help from or worked with all of her sisters, as well as her cousin Isabel Montoya Atencio. For a couple of years she worked with Tonita Roybal, and later her daughter-in-law Santana helped her. But if one considers other internationally famous potters whose signature is important to their work, one must remember that they all have scores of workers helping them at various stages of pottery-making. Why should a Pueblo Indian potter be singled out and required to do all of the work herself?

An extremely important point in regard to signatures is the fact that Maria's youngest sister, Clara Montoya, who, since she was young, has helped Maria with polishing and would at times, when she completed polishing a vessel, put Maria's signature on the bottom herself. For this reason there is a not uncommon signature on the bottom of Maria's pottery that is not Maria's own signature (Figure 4.6). The obvious differences between Clara's signature and that of Maria herself is that the *M* is printed instead of written, and there is a circle over the *i* instead of a dot. This "irregular" signature seems to have taken place only during the Marie-and-Julian period (1907–1943). As the importance of authentic signatures was increasingly realized, Clara's signing of pottery was stopped. Those vessels signed with "Marie & Julian" by Clara, however, are unquestionably Maria pottery. Maria has said

67

with regard to this signature that it is her own; that at one time she printed the *M* and put a circle over the *i* because she used a sharper polishing stone for signing. However, the better explanation seems to be that it is Clara's signature.

When Maria began working with Santana in 1943, the signature was changed to "Marie & Santana" (Figure 4.7). This signature remained unchanged until the late Marie-and-Santana period when a few pieces were signed "Maria & Santana." Richard M. Howard has in his collection a piece purchased from Popovi and Anita Da's shop in September, 1954, that bears the "Maria & Santana" signature. This would be one of the earliest pieces with the signature "Maria" rather than "Marie" and one of the few authentic pieces that are signed "Maria & Santana." After all this time, Maria finally began using her true name (Maria) rather than "Marie" on her pottery, mostly as a result of Alice Marriott's publication of the book, *María: The Potter of San Ildefonso*. People would wonder why the pottery was signed "Marie" when her name was Maria.

When Maria began working with her son, Popovi Da, in 1956, the signature then became "Maria/Popovi" (Figure 4.8), and at that time they began to distinguish between pottery that was done by Maria alone and that which was done in collaboration. When the pottery was undecorated the signature was "Maria Poveka." This signature was abandoned by the mid-1960s, however, when all pieces were signed "Maria/Popovi," decorated and undecorated alike. In 1959 Popovi Da introduced the system of adding the month and year of firing to the signature to distinguish authentic Maria pieces from other pieces that carried her name. Thus the signature became "Maria/Popovi 561" or "Maria Poveka 467," meaning the pottery was fired in April 1967.

CHAPTER FIVE

Honors and Awards

MARIA AND JULIAN RECEIVED their first public recognition in 1904 at the St. Louis World's Fair (Louisiana Purchase Exhibition) where they were invited as part of a group, mainly to perform Indian dances, but where Maria first demonstrated pottery-making in public.

Again in 1914 Maria and Julian participated at the Panama-California Exposition (San Diego World's Fair) as part of a group of potters from San Ildefonso selected by Dr. Edgar L. Hewett to demonstrate pottery-making within the pueblo constructed on the grounds of the Exposition. At this time they were only making Polychrome ware and dull Black ware for domestic use; however, it was at San Diego that Maria and Julian first succeeded in making larger vessels.

In 1934 Maria and Julian were invited as special exhibitors to the Chicago World's Fair Century of Progress, where they received special recognition by the Ford Exhibition and were awarded a bronze medal. At a special ceremony held at the Fair, Maria was awarded another bronze medal for Indian Achievement by the Indian Fire Council, a national Indian-interest organization which was the only national recognition given to Indians at that time, and has remained the highest in stature since. Maria was the second person and the first woman to receive this award. An interesting aside to Maria and Julian's presence at the Chicago World's Fair is a brief article that appeared in the Los Angeles Southwest Museum publication in 1934:

> An industrialist whose plant turns out two million pieces of pottery a year has an exhibit at the Chicago World's Fair. A building of neo-classic design devotes ten thousand feet of floor space to machinery for every process in modern pottery-making; huge mixers, conveyors, ovens generating a temperature of 2000° Fahrenheit. The exhibit is a factory in itself.

RÉPUBLIQUE FRANÇAISE.

MINISTÈRE DE L'ÉDUCATION NATIONALE.

Le Ministre de l'Éducation Nationale,

Vu l'article 32 du décret organique du 17 mars 1808;

Vu les ordonnances royales des 14 novembre 1844, 9 septembre 1845 et 1ᵉʳ novembre 1846;

Vu les décrets des 9 novembre 1850, 7 avril et 27 décembre 1866, 24 décembre 1885,

25 mars 1921, 4 février 1922, 13 septembre 1924 et 23 juin 1928.

Arrête :

Madame *Martinez* Maria

à San Ildefonso (Nouveau Mexique) Services rendus aux Arts

est nommé Officier d'Académie.

Pour ampliation :
L'Administrateur civil
chargé du bureau du Cabinet,

Fait à Paris, le 4 Août 1954

Le Ministre de l'Éducation Nationale,

Signé : Jean Berthoin

Palmes Academiques awarded to Maria in 1954 by the French Government. Photograph by Cradoc Bagshaw.

By way of impressing the visitor of the progress of the ceramic arts under modern methods, the owner had instructed an assistant to have a primitive potter at work. Whether this small detail was a mistake or a master stroke, the Chicago *Tribune* account does not say. We infer though, that Maria and Julian Martinez, Tewa Pueblo Indians and master potters of San Ildefonso in New Mexico, set amid this costly array of gleaming machinery with their dime's worth of homemade equipment and steal the show. They are artists, and machines are just machines.[1]

The Golden Gate International Exposition (San Francisco World's Fair) was held on Treasure Island in 1939 and was the last World's Fair where Maria and Julian demonstrated pottery-making.

The University of Colorado at Boulder awarded Maria Poveka Martinez a bronze medal in 1953 for having made the greatest contribution to the arts.

In 1954 the American Institute of Architects at their 86th annual convention in Boston presented to Maria Montoya Martinez their national award, The Craftsmanship Medal, the nation's highest honor for craftsmanship. The text from the award is worth repeating:

Maria receiving the Craftsmanship Medal from the American Institute of Architects in Boston in 1954. *Left to right:* Popovi Da, Maria Martinez, and Clair W. Ditchy, president of the American Institute of Architects.

In awarding to you Maria Montoya Martinez, "The Potter of San Ildefonso" The Craftsmanship Medal, the American Institute of Architects honors a daughter of a Race and land whose arts were great long before the name America was known. Rediscovering techniques lost for centuries, you have raised them to new heights, still unaided by potters wheel or closed kiln. We honor not only the skill of your hands, but also your holding fast to the Pueblo Indian's early teaching that your discoveries and the fruits of your labors were not yours to keep, but rather for sharing with all your people.

Also in 1954, at a special ceremony held at the Inter-Tribal Indian Ceremonial in Gallup, New Mexico, Maria Montoya Martinez was awarded the *Palmes Academiques* by the French Government, an honor conferred for service in the educational field; in this case, for her contributions to the arts.

Maria received yet another bronze medal in 1959, the Jane Addams Award for Distinguished Service, at a ceremony in Santa Fe. The award, presented by Dr. Leland H. Carlson, president of Rockford College, is made annually by Rockford to an outstanding woman of the nation in memory of the college's most famous graduate, Jane Addams. Maria was selected "to commemorate the devotion she had shown to her own

71

people and her great accomplishment in developing and preserving the art of her people." Previous recipients include Dr. Sarah Jordan, Director of the Leahey Clinic, and Dr. Ada Comstock, retired president of Radcliffe College and long-time dean of Smith College.

In 1960 the National Catholic Art Association presented Maria the following citation:

> Maria Montoya Martinez, of San Ildefonso Pueblo, New Mexico, is an artist in the traditional sense. Not only is she an accomplished potter, but she has done much to restore that ancient craft when it seemed doomed to oblivion. More important has been her work for her own people by means of which she has strengthened them against secularizing pressures. Though her life's work has been exceptional, she has shown no ambition to be considered an exceptional person. She has done the work that lay before her, but with great wisdom and courage. Her example should be an inspiration to all Christian workmen.

Opening on May 15, 1967, the Center for the Arts of Indian America sponsored the *Three-Generation Show* featuring the works of Maria, son Popovi Da, and grandson Tony Da. The gala exhibition was held in the United States Department of Interior building in Washington, D.C. Santa Fe, New Mexico, was fortunate enough to have a special preview of the show held at the Institute of American Indian Art, opening on April 2nd of that year.

The American Ceramic Society presented its Presidential Citation to Maria Montoya Martinez at Pasadena on October 25, 1968:

> For untiring efforts to elevate and improve the state of Indian ceramic art — the first of the American ceramic industries — for the betterment of her Pueblo and the American Indian as a whole, the President and the Board of Trustees have conferred this citation as a token of esteem.

The Minnesota Museum of Art in St. Paul presented the Symbol of Man award to Maria Poveka in December of 1969 for her contribution in reviving the ancient art of Pueblo Indian pottery-making.

In 1971 New Mexico State University at Las Cruces, New Mexico, awarded Maria Martinez an Honorary Doctorate of Fine Arts.

Maria Martinez was the national recipient of the Catlin Peace Pipe Award from the American Indian Lore Association in 1974.

Also in 1974, the New Mexico Arts Commission presented the First Annual Governor's Award to Maria Martinez for outstanding service to the arts in the field of pottery. At a ceremony at the Museum of

Albuquerque, Governor Bruce King stated that she has "brought artistic distinction and great economic benefits to her pueblo." Other recipients of this award were photographer Laura Gilpin, artist Georgia O'Keeffe, architect John Gaw Meem, art historian Dr. E. Boyd, and musician Grace Thompson Edmister.

On May 4, 1976 the National Council on Education for the Ceramic Arts presented "the title of Honorary Member of the Council in recognition of productive scholarship in education and notable contributions to the ceramic arts" to Maria and Julian Martinez.

Maria Martinez received an Honorary Doctorate Degree from Columbia College in Chicago on June 10, 1977. The Presbyterian Hospital Foundation presented Maria with the Award for Excellence for 1977. The Foundation presents this award annually to outstanding individuals who have achieved excellence in their professional pursuits. Previous recipients have been Dr. Ralph Bunche, Miss Greer Garson, Peter Hurd, Paul Horgan, and Noris Bradbury.

The foregoing list of honors and awards is not complete; such a list would be exhaustive. Maria received other honors, such as visiting the White House four times, during the administrations of Hoover, Roosevelt, Eisenhower and Johnson. Maria is listed in *Who's Who of American Women*. She has consistently won the top awards with her pottery at the annual Indian Market in Santa Fe sponsored by the Southwestern Association of Indian Affairs, and at the annual Inter-Tribal Indian Ceremonial in Gallup. Unfortunately, records of other honors are incomplete or lost.

The White House, 1967. Left to right: Popovi Da, Tony Da, Mrs. Stewart Udall, Maria Martinez, Lady Bird Johnson, and Edna Massey. Photograph by Robert L. Knudsen, The White House.

This is the Lady Bird and me; and this was the secretary [Mrs. Stewart Udall]. Her husband used to be for the Indians, a long time, that Udall. [And] Edna Massey.

     The first president I met was Roosevelt, and his wife, Mrs. Roosevelt. They were very nice at the White House.
     And then Eisenhower and Hoover.
     Johnson. And the Lady Bird came here to visit. So I asked the ladies if they can put on a dance for her, and they did. Oh, the Indian governors, lieutenant governor, everybody came! And the council man said that the Lady Bird says she wants to visit an old house and a modern house. So they, the council man, chose my sister's house, Desideria. And another house. And Desideria was scared. And she say, "Oh, the President, why is he coming to see my house? But I'm not going to show the kitchen, just the living room." But the Lady Bird didn't care. She

74

went all through the house. And she said that she was used to old houses and people. That she live in a ranch; I don't know where; Texas.

And so she was very nice. And the council man said, they had a meeting and they told the mothers not to let the kids go and bother her. But she didn't care. She go all over like [a] chicken.

And we had pictures taken in the store [Popovi Da Studio]. Po and me and the Lady Bird. And she sent me the pictures. And then she invited me to Washington. And I said, "I don't know if I go." "Well, you try and go. Won't cost you a penny." So me and Po and Tony Da, we flew up and we stayed a week . . .

While I was in Washington they took me where they were building the airport, and they said it was the largest in the world in Washington [Dulles International Airport]. So they took me out and I put my hand on the big glass. It was raining. At the airport I said [a dedication prayer] to be a place for good luck for our people in the Mother Earth and the United States. I didn't say United States but in our language. In our language, the Mother Earth and the Father Sun, to help them. To help them run this airport. And in New York I said that to the Rockefeller building . . . I support my hand and they rolled the big stone. And I am happy because they think of me, you see, and they believe that, that I am all right with everything.

And we were ready to come home the next day and then they asked me if I could stay two more days. There were some Indians coming and they wanted to visit me. And I thought those northern Indians. And I said to Po, "Shall we stay?" "Yes, you can stay," he said. So we stayed. But they weren't; they were from India. Those people were from India. But they were dressed up, oh, so pretty. And they were Indians from India. So then they made a party for us with those Indians.

MARIA

75

Figure 6.1 Black-on-black storage jar (1964); last large vessel made by Maria and decorated by Popovi, 16″ x 17″. Signature: Maria/Popovi 7-8-64. Courtesy Mr. and Mrs. Dennis Lyon, Scottsdale. Photograph by Jerry Jacka.

CHAPTER SIX

Maria and Popovi

*P*OPOVI DA IS A NAME synonymous with quality. Following the high standards already established by his parents, he succeeded in carrying the ceramic art to even higher plateaus of creativity. Many experts feel that the Maria/Popovi period expressed the highest level of Maria's genius. Certainly this is true in the introduction and refinement of firing techniques, creating new colors and combinations of colors, new finishes, and a higher level of perfection. Po was the first in a new generation of innovative potters who were not satisfied with doing the same thing over and over again. He had the inner artistic compulsion to experiment with new forms and techniques, to create individual works of art. At the same time he felt frustrated in his individual creativity. He did not want to compete with his mother, not because of any restraint put on him by Maria herself: he simply felt that his period of individual artistic expression would come after Maria's retirement, that he could then devote his full energies in his own directions. Maria was Maria, and he did not want to take even the slightest from her preeminent position. Unfortunately, that time never came. We can only conjecture what a creative flow might have come from such a period.

Although totally at ease and comfortable with all levels of non-Indian society, Popovi Da was first a Pueblo Indian. He was a ceremonial and religious leader and was elected governor of his Pueblo six times. He served as chairman of the All-Pueblo Council.

Po was also a community and business leader. He was a member of the New Mexico Arts Commission serving on the Rules Committee.

Po had a much greater influence on the whole Pueblo pottery industry than is generally realized. By maintaining the high standards of his parents, these standards were consciously or unconsciously the ones other potters emulated. He did more for Indian artists than they will ever know or appreciate. He encouraged and gained for them the opportunity to participate in Southwest arts and crafts shows, some of which were previously for all intents and purposes for non-Indians only. He further encouraged excellence among all Pueblo potters by arranging for quality pieces to be recognized with prizes and ribbons. Being an eloquent speaker, his many talks throughout the nation helped to educate the public not only about the pottery of his family and pueblo, but that of leading potters of other pueblos too. More than once aspiring young potters were complimented when Po would stop at their booth at Indian Market and purchase one of their pieces.

A good friend tells the following story about Po:

> Mrs. Simmons down in southern New Mexico was a great admirer of Indians and of Indian crafts in spite of the fact that she had been through the last of the Apache raids in southern New Mexico. She lived in a little poverty stricken house, watching her pennies carefully. She had many friends, including the Taylors who lived on a small ranch on the way to Silver City. In November one year I had a letter from Marian Taylor enclosing a check for five dollars and asking me to buy a Maria pot for a Christmas present for Mrs. Simmons. Marian wrote that Mrs. Simmons had always wanted to own a piece of Maria's pottery and now the Taylors wanted to give her one. Would I please buy a jar and send it to them? Well, check in hand, I went out to San Ildefonso to deal with Po. I explained the situation, told Po of Mrs. Simmons' admiration for all things Indian and of her wish to own a piece of his mother's work and of her inability to buy anything at all but absolute necessities. "I don't want to send just an ash tray," I told him. "It must be something that is really nice. Let's see what you have and I'll pay the difference." Po rummaged around and brought out three medium size ollas. He lined them up on the counter and I chose one. "How much is this one?" I asked. "Five dollars," said Po, straight faced. "Oh no you don't," I protested. "I know better than that. How much???" Po said, "It isn't very often that an Indian can do something for a white person except with their hands. It's five dollars."

It was not until after Po's death in 1971 that the prices on outstanding Indian pottery escalated so rapidly. Po had set what he felt was a fair but modest price on his and Maria's pottery. After his death, when he could no longer control the prices on Maria/Popovi pottery, the prices soared to ten times what they had been. At the same time the prices on the work of other leading potters soared. After all, before this they were not able to charge more for one of their pots than the price of a Maria.

Maria and Popovi.

Maria, Julian, and Popovi Da (c.1925).

Po liked to play with the kids outside, and one of my uncles used to say, "Don't let him play like that, hanging in those branches, swinging. He's going to spoil himself . . ." And I said to my uncle, "But he likes that." And he said, "Send him to round up the cows. You have so little cows and they're scattered up." "But he don't know," I say. He start learning how to play Tarzan, like Tarzan.

And Adam was a farmer since little boy.

And John liked to study. John liked to look at books and study and read and go to school. He was the one that went to Stanford to school. And he was a football player. And I said to him, "That play I don't like. I see so many get hurt. Here they come bleeding." And he said, "No, Mother. I take care of myself." That was John.

And Po, now Po he sometime, if he feel like it, he go and round the cows, the little we had. If he get tired, he just come home.

And Adam, now, he worked, and the Spanish people used to tell me, "Don't you let him work hard. He's going to be short." And that's the way it happened. Adam, he's short. And all the three are big boys. But no girls. So they were happy. We were all happy.

Phillip, he was just a boy. But the first time he went to Navy, when they [had] war. He was in California, that Phillip. Po was too in Army, and John was in the Army. But not Adam.

[When Po was older] he liked to play and he liked to dance, social dances, playing dances. No ceremony. And one of my nephew used to call Po, all that dancing, how they say that? — dancing feet. Dancing feet, one of my nephew used to say, Anna's boy. And he said, he's just like Tarzan. But he was not a good farmer.

He started with the pottery when he got married, but before that he was a painter. He started painting birds and little animals . . . When he marry, then he start on pottery. Painting and building [pottery], helping me to fire.

And his father used to say, "Go ahead and think like a man and build your house." So we gave him a lot, big lot. And afterward he got interested in pottery. Then every piece that when we fire, he say, "I'm going to keep this one, Mamma." "All right. Go ahead." And so they have a lot of my pottery. Some pretty ones. Whichever pots he liked he said, "I'm going to take this." "All right."

And afterward he got interested in pottery, Po. Then he don't want to sleep. He just go ahead and paint [pottery]. We fired in two days, big lot . . . but he helped me a lot, firing, getting ready the clay. He helped me get the clay over the mountains. They have pictures where we went with Po to get the clay, that Po digs out the clay . . . and then soak them, and then he's the one that mix the clay, and I make the pot, and then he fix them the way he want the top. And then I fix them and he sandpaper and I smooth them, and then polish them. And he put, try and put the design. And I used to say to him, "Don't take that good one. Take one small one. If you spoil it, it's not so much." But afterward he was very good. Uh-huh, he was very good. But Tony is the best one.

MARIA

81

Popovi Da Studio of Indian Art at San Ildefonso. Po and his wife, Anita, are examining one of the Maria/Popovi jars. Photograph by Laura Gilpin.

Popovi Da was born Antonio Martinez, but legally changed his name in 1948 to his Indian name, Popovi Da, which translates in English to Red Fox. In the early thirties he studied art at the Santa Fe Indian School (later to become the Institute of American Indian Art) under Dorothy Dunn. By the end of that decade his mode of expression was well defined in the "traditional" two-dimensional style, his favorite subject being animals, especially skunks.

It was not until he returned from the Army after World War II that he became seriously interested in pottery. About 1948 or 1949 he started helping Maria with digging clay and gathering temper. In addition he collected dung from the range for fuel in firing and at times helped with the firing when Adam was away.

About 1948 Popovi and Anita Da opened the Popovi Da Studio of Indian Art at San Ildefonso Pueblo to display some of Maria's exceptional pieces for public viewing and to sell outstanding examples of Indian arts and crafts as well as Maria's work.

By 1950 he began to help with the painting and decorating of Maria's pottery. Often Santana would outline the design and Po would fill in the spaces.

In 1956 Maria suggested that Po take over as a full partner, as his father had done before him. He was now working in all stages of pottery-making. The joint signature of Maria/Popovi appeared on all pieces.

Po began experimenting with Polychrome ware in 1956, a pottery type that had been almost totally abandoned just after 1925, after the introduction and instant popularity of Black-on-black ware. He entered his first perfect Polychrome piece at the Gallup Ceremonial in 1957 and won Best in Class (Figure 6.7).

In 1961 he began experiments in the firing technique that resulted in a new color: sienna. It was a two-firing process. After first firing the pottery black, the pottery was then refired without the smoking process, thus burning off the carbon. The resulting color was sienna (Figures 6.15 and 6.16).

By 1964 Po developed yet another new type: Black-and-sienna ware (Figures 6.17, 6.18, and 6.23). Po would never say how he achieved both colors on one vessel, except that it was a two-firing process. The following observation made by Guthe in 1921 gives a strong hint as to how the result was achieved:

> Certain polished black vessels are further manipulated in such a way as to produce an irregular red blotch upon them. (This variant in polished black ware is a new departure. It was discovered, probably accidentally, by one of the San Ildefonso potters early in the summer of 1921. The process by which the red blotch is made has not as yet been brought completely under control.) Specimens destined to receive this red blotch, which is usually placed near the rim, are reburied in the hot manure lying round the edge of the pile with that portion which is to have the blotch left uncovered. Against this exposed portion is placed a smoking fragment of a dung-slab. The action of the heat and air results in the removal of the carbon from the surface, so that that part of the vessel which is not covered with manure and ashes regains its former color, the red of the pigment. Since the pot is pushed about a good deal during this process, the line between the red and the black surface is not always very definite, which improves the appearance. The Indians themselves cannot tell beforehand just what shape the blotch is going to take, and must therefore watch the vessel continually. Sometimes burning sherds of cedar bark are placed against the exposed surface to hasten the process, but actual flames are not necessary in order to obtain

Figure 6.2   Black-on-black water jar (1967); feather design, 12″ x 14″. Signature: Maria/ Popovi 1167. Courtesy Mr. and Mrs. Dennis Lyon, Scottsdale. Photograph by Jerry Jacka.

Figure 6.3   Black-on-black plate (1965); stylized skunk design, 6″ diameter. Signature: Maria/Popovi 565. Courtesy Mr. and Mrs. Dennis Lyon, Scottsdale. Photograph by Jerry Jacka.

the desired result. If the red blotch is too large, part of it is simply recovered with hot manure-ashes, and a few minutes later will again become jet black. So far as looks are concerned the success or failure of this red blotch upon black ware depends largely upon the artistic sense of the potter making it. In one group of thirty-three polished black vessels fired together, sixteen were given a red blotch; eight or ten of these were excellent pieces.[1]

Po's technique must have been a refinement of this process. In a second controlled firing, he would burn off the black in the areas he desired to be the sienna color.

One of the most popular new finishes developed by Po was Gunmetal ware (Figure 6.4). This was achieved by firing in the same manner as for Black ware but in a hotter and longer fire. The process required a greater firing skill for if the pottery was taken out too soon it would be regular Black ware, and if left in an instant too long it would be overfired and consequently dull gray instead of the desired shiny gunmetal. The only other potter to master this firing technique has been Santana.

The first piece signed "Popovi" (alone) appeared in 1965. The *Maria/Popovi* pottery was made by Maria and decorated by Po, but the *Popovi* pieces were made by Po alone. Po expressed form in his creations, and the results were exciting. Few such pieces were made and are now considered rare collectors' items (Figures 6.22 and 6.23).

Po was the first contemporary Pueblo potter to add turquoise to his work. His original idea was to use a small piece of turquoise set on the pottery as a hallmark. However, he quickly abandoned the idea.

Po gave considerable credit to Anna O. Shepard for encouraging and aiding him with her invaluable and incomparable knowledge of pueblo ceramics. She encouraged him to work on a revival of Glaze ware, which had not been done since the seventeenth century. He experimented in Glaze ware but never perfected a piece to his satisfaction.

If Po had not been working closely with Maria, she probably would have retired in the early 1960s. With her advancing years, pottery-making became increasingly difficult. She no longer made large pieces, and even the small pieces became heavier in contrast to the fine, thin-walled pottery of earlier years. During the last few years Po would straighten some of the pottery before it began to dry, since it was not always totally symmetrical. Maria did retire from pottery-making in November 1970, although she continues at times to demonstrate the making of a small piece which is left unfinished.

Figure 6.4 Gunmetal bowls and jar. Left to right, *a*. Plain, polished, closed black bowl (1965) with Gunmetal firing, 2½″ x 3″. Signature: Maria Poveka, 365. *b*. Plain, polished, closed black bowl (1970) with Gunmetal firing. Signature: Maria/Popovi 1270. *c*. Plain, polished black bowl (1969) with Gunmetal firing, 2½″ x 3½″. Signature: Maria/Popovi 769. *d*. Plain, polished black jar (1967) with Gunmetal firing, 7″ x 7¾″. Signature: Maria Poveka 467. *e*. Plain, polished black bowl (1970) with Gunmetal firing, 3½″ x 4¼″. Signature: Maria/Popovi 870. Private Collection. Photograph by Jerry Jacka.

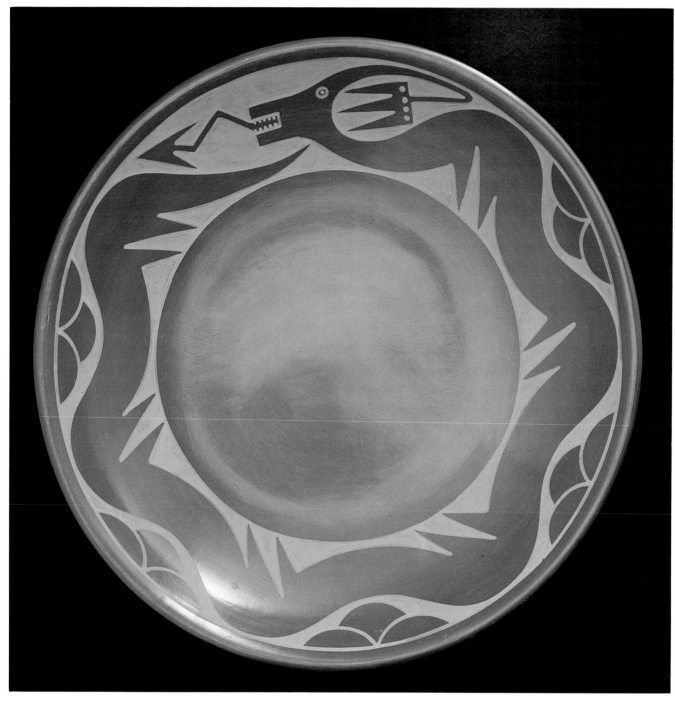

Figure 6.5 Buff-on-red plate (1966); *avanyu* design, 15″ diameter. Signature: Maria/Popovi 1266. Courtesy Mr. and Mrs. Dennis Lyon, Scottsdale. Photograph by Jerry Jacka.

Figure 6.6   Buff-on-red jar (1965); feather design with Mother Earth/Father Sky, 8¼″ x 9″. Signature: Maria/Popovi 1265. Courtesy Mr. and Mrs. Dennis Lyon, Scottsdale. Photograph by Jerry Jacka.

Figure 6.7   Polychrome plate (1957); Po's first successful Polychrome, entered at Gallup
Inter-Tribal Ceremonial in 1957: Best in Show Award; 14" diameter. Signature: Maria/
Popovi. Courtesy Da Collection, San Ildefonso. Photograph by Jerry Jacka.

Figure 6.8   Polychrome water jar (1966); an elaborate use of feather, floral, and geometric motifs, 9¼" x 10¾". Signature: Maria/Popovi 866. Courtesy Da Collection, San Ildefonso. Photograph by Jerry Jacka.

Figure 6.9   Polychrome plate (1969); feather and *avanyu* designs, 15" diameter. Signature: Maria/Popovi 569. Courtesy Da Collection, San Ildefonso. Photograph by Jerry Jacka.

Figure 6.10 Polychrome plate (1966); detailed use of geometric designs, 11¾″ diameter.
Signature: Maria/Popovi 766. Private Collection. Photograph by Jerry Jacka.

Figure 6.11   Polychrome plate (1959); skunk design incorporating sun, rain, mountain, rainbow, and cloud motifs, 13½″ diameter. Signature: Maria/Popovi 859. Courtesy Da Collection, San Ildefonso. Photograph by Jerry Jacka.

94

Figure 6.12 Polychrome water jar (1958); an early Maria/Popovi Polychrome with a lavish use of detail reminiscent of the style of Julian, 9½″ x 10¾″. Signature: Maria/Popovi. Private Collection. Photograph by Jerry Jacka.

Figure 6.13   Polychrome shallow bowl (1966); squash blossom design, 2½″ x 10⅛″. Signature: Maria/Popovi 666. Collection of author, Santa Fe. Photograph by Cradoc Bagshaw.

Figure 6.14 Polychrome "Snake Pot" (c. 1960); a Maria/Popovi jar painted by Po in the style of the famous Maria & Julian "Snake Pot," 9" x 9½". Signature: Maria/Popovi. Courtesy Da Collection, San Ildefonso. Photograph by Laura Gilpin.

Figure 6.15   Sienna plate (1964); feather design, 11⅜'' diameter. Signature: Maria/Popovi 664. Courtesy Mr. and Mrs. Dennis Lyon, Scottsdale. Photograph by Jerry Jacka.

Figure 6.16 Sienna jar (1964); *avanyu* design with deer tracks encircling neck and cloud design at top of neck, 13½" x 9¼". Signature: Maria/Popovi 664. Courtesy Da Collection, San Ildefonso. Photograph by Jerry Jacka.

Figure 6.17 Black-and-sienna plate (1969); stylized fish, painted and incised design, one of the few times Po did incising, 10¾" diameter. Signature: Maria/Popovi 669. Courtesy Mr. and Mrs. Peter Hirsch, Santa Fe. Photograph by Jerry Jacka.

100

Figure 6.18   Black-and-sienna jar (1966); feather design, 5½″ x 7½″. Signature: Maria/
Popovi 566. Courtesy Mr. and Mrs. Russ Lyon, Jr., Scottsdale. Photograph by Jerry Jacka.

Figure 6.19   Polished black water jar (1963); double-shouldered plain black polished jar, 11¾″ x 10″. Signature: Maria Poveka 1063. Courtesy Mr. and Mrs. Dennis Lyon, Scottsdale. Photograph by Jerry Jacka.

Figure 6.20   Polished red jar (1957); plain polished red jar, 9¾" x 9¼." Signature: Maria Poveka. Private Collection. Photograph by Jerry Jacka.

Figure 6.21   Black-on-black storage jar (c. 1940), *avanyu* and cloud designs, 15″ x 18½″.
Signature: Marie & Julian. The elegant simplicity of this jar makes it a classic. Originally
purchased by Jacques Cartier of Pojoaque, New Mexico; Mr. Cartier liked to tell the story of
how Maria carried the jar on her back from San Ildefonso to his home in Pojoaque, some 6
miles. Anita Da clearly remembers delivering the jar with Popovi Da in their vehicle, however. Courtesy Mr. Anthony Pedone, New York, NY. Photograph by Jerry Jacka.

Figure 6.22   Polished black jar (1967); plain polished black double-shouldered jar with an
unusual shape, 12″ x 11″. Signature: Popovi 467. Courtesy Da Collection, San Ildefonso.
Photograph by Jerry Jacka.

Figure 6.23 Black-and-sienna jar with lid (1967); *avanyu* design, turquoise inset in lid, 13″ x 10″. Signature: Popovi 1067. Courtesy Mr. and Mrs. Peter Hirsch, Santa Fe. Photograph by Jerry Jacka.

Figure 6.25   Incised black jar with lid (c. 1969); *avanyu* design, 8″ x 6¼″. Signature: DA.
Courtesy Da Collection, San Ildefonso. Photograph by Jerry Jacka.

Po was extremely proud of his son Tony Da, the third generation of the Martinez family. A noted painter as well as a potter, other than studying under Josef Bakos* during high school, he had no formal training as an artist, but had tutelage in ceramics by both his father and grandmother. His artistic talent was recognized early when at the age of sixteen he won first place in a Hallmark card contest.

Entering his paintings in the Gallup Inter-Tribal Ceremonial in 1967, Tony won every conceivable award. Flo Wilkes, writing in the Albuquerque *Journal* (July 9, 1967), stated "Tony has emerged as an exciting young painter, combining traditional Indian art with contemporary concepts, creating his own professional style."

After leaving the Navy in 1964, Tony lived with Maria for six years. It was at this time that his artistic skill in ceramics developed. Returning from the *Three Generation Show* in Washington, D.C., in 1967, he began to work on his first ceramic sculptures, creating an exciting new form of Pueblo ceramic art (Figures 6.27-6.29).

Tony was the first to popularize the use of turquoise on pottery, sometimes using a single stone in a simple, pleasing manner, and often using turquoise elaborately inlaid to give contrast in color and texture to the pottery clay (Figures 6.27-6.30). He was also the first to incise designs on his vessels.† Beginning with the traditional *avanyu*, his design concepts have grown over the years to elaborate and detailed designs combined with the use of turquoise, coral and shell stones and heishi, and later silver lids (Figure 6.30). For this book Tony made the following statement about his work:

> People often approach me and ask why they don't see much of my pottery today. The simple truth is that I originally started as a painter, and working with pottery came later, quite by accident. Although my brief encounter with ceramics has been exceptionally lucrative, I must admit that painting is my first love and line of endeavor I hope to pursue in the future.
>
> Abstract designs such as geometric and parallel lines have always been intriguing and have held a strange fascination for me. My first introduction to the realm of the abstract

---

*Internationally known artist Joseph Bakos was one of Santa Fe's *Cinco Pintores*, a group of five prominent Santa Fe artists that first established that city's art colony.

†This is to be distinguished from the San Juan incised which was a revival of the archaeological ware, Potsuwi'i Incised, led by Rose Cata of San Juan Pueblo in the 1930s. There has been discussion as to the proper term to describe this contemporary form of decoration used by such potters as Tony Da, Grace Medicine Flower, and Joseph Lonewolf. Various authorities have used the following terms: incised, etched, intaglio, and sgraffito. There has been no clear decision as to the preferred term.

Tony Da. Photograph by Jerry Jacka.

Figure 6.24   Polished black bowl with sienna sculpture on lid (1969); covered black bowl with incised handprint design; bear sculpture serves as handle on lid, 7¼″ x 7″. Signature: DA. Courtesy Mr. and Mrs. Peter Hirsch, Santa Fe. Photograph by Jerry Jacka.

The three generations: Maria, Po, and Tony. Photograph by Laura Gilpin.

was through a one-man show by Sioux artist Oscar Howe in Santa Fe when I was quite young. My particular interpretation of art may not fall into this category, but I find abstraction particularly challenging because of its infinite possibilities. Perhaps this also explains why speculation about time, space, and man's position in the universe has always been a preoccupation of mine. I only can wish my work will remain in the future as a cultural testimony to these times.

Julian with young Tony Da.

He was mostly with me at my house, Tony. So he learned more.

It was Po's idea to open the shop. After he sold a lot of pottery, and old pieces, then he began to clean up that place. And afterward he fix another one. Then we go to Arizona, buy pots, baskets from the Indians. And we go Oklahoma with Po.

[Po and Anita] were the ones that run the shop. But they got every pot I made, they got the best ones. [Po and Anita purchased these pots from Maria at the time.] Books and medals I got from all over . . .

[When Po wanted to open the shop] I said to him, "Go ahead, if you want to be a man and take care of it. That's nothing like play," I said. "You'll have to work like a man." "I do it, I do it." So he start, and he was very good, too.

After he quit Los Alamos; he worked at Los Alamos, and then he went to Army, and when he came from Army then he start hard on the shop. Then he got interest, interest in it. And all the time taking good pots [for the museum at the Popovi Da Studio] when we fire: "I'm going to keep this."

But my oldest son [Adam], he's a good worker.

But he's always a big boy [Po], not like Adam. And John is a big boy, too. And Phillip. They all three big boys. Just Adam. But the Span-ish people, neighbors used to say, "Don't make him work too hard, that boy's going to stay small." And he did. But he like to work on the field. But not John nor Po nor Phillip.

They used to take John, at the military school in Atlanta, Georgia. He's the only one who went to school out. Po did, but not much.

And now I have about thirty-four great-grandchildren. And about nineteen great-great. And two more to come. And my own [grandchil-dren], just twelve. Just twelve, but now the other, the grandchildren, great-grandchildren, and then the great-great grandchildren. And they take, oh, a big cake, too, for my birthday. And we invite them, the kids; [they come] just like little chickens [running all around].

MARIA

113

The young dancer; Tony Da (c.1945). Photograph by Laura Gilpin.

And their son [Po's and Anita's son, Tony Da], he grew up with me. And he was still watching how I make pottery, that Tony. And I say to him, "Don't play with the clay like your dad. Go ahead and make good pottery." And he was interested in pottery. But not John. Adam either. Adam didn't make pottery, but see, sandpaper now and help fire, to get ready for firing and all.

And Tony Da used to stay with me when he was young. I think after the Navy for a long time. That's when I, when he used [to stay], when I make pottery and he try to make pottery. And he say, "Don't cook, Grandma, I'm going to get some hamburger[s]." And since that I don't like hamburger. Maybe is too much for me. It was all the time hamburger. He don't want me to stop making pottery. He want to get hamburger. And I said, "That Tony spoil me too much." So I don't eat hamburger anymore.

MARIA

115

Figure 6.26   Incised Black-and-sienna plate (c. 1970); bison design, 13″ diameter. Signature: DA. Courtesy Mr. and Mrs. Dennis Lyon, Scottsdale. Photograph by Jerry Jacka.

116

Figure 6.27   Incised Black-and-sienna sculpture (1970); turtle sculpture with incised *avanyu* design set with 9 turquoise stones, 5½" x 10". Signature: DA. Courtesy Mr. and Mrs. Dennis Lyon, Scottsdale. Photograph by Jerry Jacka.

117

Figure 6.28   Incised Black-and-sienna sculpture (c. 1970); owl sculpture, 9½″ x 12″ wing span. Signature: DA. Mr. and Mrs. Peter Hirsch, Santa Fe. Photograph by Jerry Jacka.

Figure 6.29   Bear fetishes. *Left,* natural bear fetish (c. 1974); unpolished bear sculpture with key design and turquoise inset to work with heart-line design, 6″ x 9¼″. Signature: DA. Courtesy Mr. and Mrs. E. D. Obrecht, Phoenix. *Middle,* Black-and-sienna bear fetish (1968) in which a sienna medallion is surrounded by channeled turquoise, 7½″ x 5″. Signature: DA. Courtesy Mr. and Mrs. Dennis Lyon, Scottsdale. *Right,* red bear fetish (1973) with an intricate key design around center of body divided by turquoise and shell heishe; heart-line design set off by inset turquoise, 6½″ x 10½″. Signature: DA. Courtesy Mr. and Mrs. Dennis Lyon, Scottsdale. Photograph by Jerry Jacka.

119

Figure 6.30   Red stone-polished jar with lid (1972); elaborate turtle and *avanyu* design set with turquoise and shell heishi around base of neck, elaborate sculpted lid set with turquoise and heishi, 7¼″ x 4⅞″. Signature: DA. Private Collection. Photograph by Jerry Jacka.

Figure 6.31   Black-and-sienna jar (1970); "Three Generation Pot" made, finished, and fired by Maria and Popovi. Tony Da completed the incised *avanyu* design and added the turquoise and shell heishi. It is intended that Tony add his signature to the bottom of this pot. This is the only pot done by all three generations together. 8½" x 8¾". Signature: Maria/Popovi 1070. Courtesy Da Collection, San Ildefonso. Photograph by Jerry Jacka.

Bernard Leach and Shoji Hamada* were present at the opening of the new Museum of International Folk Art in Santa Fe in 1952. It was during this visit that they had the opportunity to meet Maria. Bernard Leach recalls that meeting in a tape addressed to Maria Martinez and Anita Da in July, 1977:

I'm so glad in a way, especially now, to talk to anybody in that family, just personally, because I gather that Maria is now at my age, just about. I am just over ninety, and I can still talk, as you can see. And I'm glad to say something in memory of that meeting which I've never forgotten, with not only Maria Martinez, at a visit to San Ildefonso, and of her visit to the new Museum of International Folk Art, to which Hamada and Yanagi and I spoke the very first lecture on our visit in 1952, I think, all that time ago. The memory has been vivid. I made contact. I will describe it again a little bit, so that it may come back as a link between us, and between me and Maria. I felt I met the Indian people in that Pueblo of San Ildefonso.

I was taken by a kind American lady, Laura Gilpin, and we went to see Maria and could not find her. And before we left, as it was getting cold with snow on the ground, I said, "Wait a minute, please, while I look round the horizon for smoke." And smoke I saw, coming gently from behind one of those buildings, and I said, "Let's go behind and see what is the cause of that smoke." And there stood Maria, and I and my companions watched at a little distance, whilst our friend went to talk to her and to introduce us.

And she came towards us and talked, and said she was unpacking or cooling . . . once they were cooling, open firing without the kiln, of the pots she had made entirely by hand as I saw her do later on. And I was mesmerized by the ease and the speed with which she handled clay, polished clay, prepared it, waited for one while the light from the redness, its redness in the ashes, died away. And she finally hooked it out with a piece of iron, and we saw how American Indians had made one kind of blackware, which was smoked, so as the red color of the clay became black, and some pots were polished while the clay was still damp, and other pots were made matte black, the polished part went shiny. It made a strong impression on both my two Japanese friends and myself.

And so before we left I said to her, "Would you care to come to our lecture which is, I think, to be the following night, or two nights later, at the new Museum of International Folk Art," which was opening with our lecture, talk about our

*English potter Bernard Leach and Japanese potter Shoji Hamada are recognized as the supreme masters of clay in modern times.

potting and our travel, and our foregathering of craftsmen from all over the world at Darkington Hall, which was the first of its kind.

To my delight she agreed at once that she would like to come and bring Popovi Da. She came, and it was my place to introduce — in English, of course — our three people to the full house in which the only two Indian people present, as far as I knew, were Maria and her son. And nobody was next to them. So I stepped down from the stage and went and sat next to her while she welcomed me and leant toward the stage, gazing at Hamada beginning to throw, I think on a wheel, in a simple primitive way which she could understand thoroughly well; and she was obviously engrossed. I saw her mouth open in astonishment at what she saw. This was a delight to me, but not so great as when she touched my leg and said, "Why didn't you tell us? Why didn't you tell us? Please come back to us; anything you want." In fact she was opening the doors of friendship, and I knew it, and we all knew it. And we did come back. And I did sit down . . . and I think we had some tea. I've forgotten. But we talked in intimacy, and this is a delight. She even gave me some of her polishing stones, which the men of the tribe gather at some place not very far away, I think in the mountains, which are good for polishing soft, or half-soft clay.

Well, that was one of those moments when we three, in unison, desired and managed to break down the barriers to make friendship between our people, our White people and your Red people. This is what we want, and then this is what we still want. This is the way towards the friendship between people, which may bring us peace, and peace is indeed still further off now than it was then. And we are in great need, and know it, and the more people who know it and desire what we desire, the more hope there is for the future. We want the future of all men in unity.

May I send you belatedly all my greetings, and if my friend Yanagi was alive, he would join with me, I know. Hamada is alive,* and yesterday only I heard that a fortnight ago he was perfectly well and still going on making pots, in his eighties.

Oh, I remember your countryside. That stern, rocky, eroded landscape. Oh, how I remember it! My, what I was moved by in America! There was great generosity, yes; and openness of mind, yes. But that quality that is specially of the original inhabitants, and of your people of New Mexico, I send you such warm greetings that still beat in my heart, and I know still beat in my friend Hamada's. God bless you all.

---

*Hamada died on January 5, 1978.

123

A word about myself, perhaps, before I close this. Of course, I can't do any pots myself, because at ninety I cannot see. Oh, I can just see about four per cent of what is before my eyes. But thank God I see better with my heart than I could formerly, and it still beats. Aah, I did many drawings. I've just had an exhibition at one of the two big museums in London: Victoria and Albert. And to my astonishment it has been a great success. Many thousand people came to see it. And there were many of my life's work from various parts, whether drawing and writing, and potting, and etching; all these things were there. And many people have come to talk to me all this way down, three hundred miles away at the tail end of England, about the things they care about, which is towards the unity of mankind.

There I stop sending you these warmest greetings. It was so nice to meet and talk with that very sweet woman, Maria Martinez. Farewell.

Bernard Leach
St. Ives, England
July, 1977

Maria has seen great changes at San Ildefonso during her lifetime. Since her youth, San Ildefonso has grown from a small, remote, relatively obscure, and economically poor pueblo with a dying arts and crafts tradition. Today it is located adjacent to a main state highway and has a growing population that is relatively affluent due to a revival of the arts and crafts tradition, especially in pottery. This revival has given San Ildefonso the position of being one of the Pueblo Indian arts and crafts centers in the Southwest. Maria has been the guiding spirit throughout these developments. Working with Julian then with Santana and later with Popovi Da, she first led the pottery revival and then set the tone of excellence that not only has made her the most famous of Indian potters, but has made her one of the great potters of the world.

Maria Martinez, Shoji Hamada, and Bernard Leach (1952). Photograph by Laura Gilpin.

Hamada came with Dr. Leach. I don't know what year [1952], but they asked me if they could watch me work on pottery. So I said yes, sure, and Po say yes. And so, "Well, you come tomorrow. Today we are busy, but you come tomorrow." And they came and we took them to the place where we get the clay. Then brought them home and I made some, and I made pottery.

"And when will this be finished?"

"Oh, I think will be finished by Saturday."

So they stayed in Santa Fe. Every morning at 8:00 they came to watch me. And we were getting ready to fire for Saturday. Then it snow. So [Po came over] and he said, "Oh, it's too bad it snow." And I didn't cover the place where we fire. So he went out and he cleaned up a little place . . . and then they took a picture of me and that Hamada, and Dr. Leach.

San Ildefonso Bow and Arrow Dance. Maria is the drummer (c.1969).
Photograph by Laura Gilpin.

I'm still glad that they still, some of them, use the old way. I don't want them to leave the old way, to keep on.

The young people that make in the wheel? Now, that part I don't like it. No, I wish they could use their own, you see. I was asked, oh, many times, to try the wheel. But I never did. In Chicago, they said, "You've got good hands. I think you can work with the wheel. Why don't you try it?" And I said, "Oh, if I try the wheel maybe the museum people will not like it." Because they are the ones that interest me in the pottery. And it's not nice, I think. So I won't try. I'd rather make my own way.

[Some] try the wheel. But I said, "Oh, you better not try the wheel. Try your own. Don't make on the wheel. Don't try. Make your own way. This is more valuable to us than to be in the wheel, us Indian."

The young people, oh, some of them they try hard, you see, and some of them they set it and they make it fast. They don't take, some of them, they don't have patience. They want to go ahead, be more fast.

Everything we have to have patience, for everything. And I, that's what I said to the younger people. Go ahead and work slowly. You get good pottery. And not work hard, not work fast. Then it comes out right, nice.

MARIA

CHAPTER SEVEN

The Legend, the Legacy

*A*S HAS ALREADY BEEN RELATED, Maria's pottery-making career began in 1907 with the advent of Edgar L. Hewett, who directed the archaeological excavations on the Pajarito Plateau, a short distance from San Ildefonso Pueblo. Working under the auspices of the School of American Research, the archaeologists uncovered pottery of the ancient Pajaritan culture. Maria and Julian, who were present at the site, were asked if they could reproduce some of these vessels. Thus began the now-legendary story of Maria and Julian Martinez.

The story, as is too often told, is full of misinformation. Many writers and museum exhibition catalogs relate how Maria and Julian were encouraged to reproduce the Black or Black-on-black pottery found on the Pajarito Plateau. This is entirely fiction. In order to set the record straight once and for all, we will discuss the types of pottery that were found on the Pajarito Plateau and the types of pottery that Maria produced early in her career.

Pajaritan ceramics differ from all others of the Southwest in both technology and decoration. Pajaritan potters were singularly expert in the handling of the characteristic techniques (Kidder 1915:417), and geographical isolation was such as to induce a definite homogeneous cultural development. A specimen of pottery from the region so distinctly reflects the culture in which it was produced that it is as unmistakable to the trained eye as anything Greek, Etruscan, or Egyptian (Hewett 1938, revised 1953:17).

There were basically five types of pottery found in the excavations: Glaze Paint ware, culinary ware, what is commonly referred to as Biscuit ware, Potsuwi'i Incised ware, and Sankawi Black-on-cream ware.

Glaze Paint ware. This type was probably introduced from the Zuni area during the fourteenth and fifteenth centuries. The color of the paste

127

varies depending on the amount of heat applied in firing; it can be reddish, tending to yellows and grays, while the brick-red slip is sometimes fawn or brown from over-firing. The slip is decorated with glaze paint, which is the result of the vitrification of a flux. This paint is not suitable for fine lines or lines requiring sharpness or accuracy, and thus influenced the selection of designs, since hatching and small figures could not be drawn. Designs can be obscured by the running and spreading of the paint, to the extent that they are illegible. The decoration on the redware, therefore, is characterized by large figures and the absence of detail. This type was relatively scarce on the Pajarito Plateau.

Maria and Julian never attempted Glaze Paint ware. However, shapes and design elements could have served as inspiration for pieces done by them in Polychrome. Working with Anna Shepherd, Popovi Da experimented with Glaze Paint ware in later years, but never achieved any results that he considered to be satisfactory.

Culinary ware. This type was made from poor-grade clay, full of sand or tiny quartz pebbles. Occasionally corrugated, but with the coils partially obliterated, it represented the deterioration of an earlier and finer corrugated form. Culinary ware was also done with micaceous clay, sometimes with a mica wash. Although occasionally referred to as Blackware, it was not Blackware in the true sense, in that the black was caused by smudging from use in a cooking fire rather than being fired black. This is not at all the type of Blackware associated with Maria; she never attempted making this type of crude, roughly smoothed, and inferior pottery.

Biscuit ware. This is the pottery type that, more than any other, Hewett encouraged Maria to use as a model for her work. Biscuit ware is subdivided into Biscuit A and Biscuit B. Although Biscuit A is an earlier ware, the real distinction between the two is that Biscuit A is decorated only on the interior of the bowls, while Biscuit B has decoration on both the interior and exterior surfaces. A later type-designation by H.P. Mera is Abiquiu Black-on-gray for Biscuit A, and Bandelier Black-on-gray for Biscuit B.

Biscuit ware is the characteristic pottery type and the type most commonly found on the Pajarito Plateau (Kidder 1915:419). It is distinguished from other light-colored wares of the Southwest by its peculiar yellow and gray tones and by the lightness and softness of the paste. The paste is yellowish gray, somewhat granular and porous. The temper, when it occasionally occurs, is bits of water-worn quartz. All surfaces are slipped in a color that ranges from lemon yellow to dark gray; light gray is the most common color, and it is never pure white. The slip is stone polished, but never to a high degree. Decorations are in a sharp, clear, black matte carbon paint, typically geometric with upper and lower banding (Figures 7.1-7.6).

TYPICAL POTTERY FROM THE PAJARITO PLATEAU

Above: Figure 7.1   Bandelier Black-on-gray. Excavated by Edgar L. Hewett. Museum of New Mexico Catalog No. 21213/11.
Right: Figure 7.2   Bandelier Black-on-gray. Excavated by Edgar L. Hewett. Museum of New Mexico Catalog No. 21211/11.

Left: Figure 7.3   Bandelier Black-on-gray. Museum of New Mexico Catalog No. 21515/11.
Above: Figure 7.4   Bandelier Black-on-gray. Museum of New Mexico Catalog No. 21606/11.

Above: Figure 7.5   Bandelier Black-on-gray. Museum of New Mexico Catalog No. 42928/11.
Right: Figure 7.6   Abiquiu Black-on-gray. Museum of New Mexico Catalog No. 42929/11.

All pottery courtesy Museum of New Mexico. Photographs by Herbert Lotz.

Potsuwi'i Incised ware. This ware is technically close to Biscuit ware, and is the same paste and seldom tempered. It has a lightness and softness similar to that of Biscuit ware. Unlike Biscuit ware, however, it is thin-walled and unslipped, which results in a dull gray surface with an occasional mica wash. Rectilinear geometric designs of a uniform style are incised with an instrument having a blunt point. There is no evidence of Maria having ever attempted this form. Potsuwi'i Incised ware served, however, as the inspiration for the San Juan pottery revival in the 1930s led by Rosa Cata.

Sankawi Black-on-cream ware. This type, although sparsely represented, would have also served as a model for the early pieces Maria was asked to make. A slightly later type than Biscuit ware, it was similar in style, but with a generally finer design treatment. It can be quite similar in appearance to Biscuit ware.

Maria and Julian's earliest work was in Polychrome, as that was the prevailing San Ildefonso form at that time. The pieces she made beginning in 1907, when she was encouraged by Hewett to use Pajaritan pottery as her inspiration, were all done in Polychrome. There was no Pajaritan Black pottery, other than the crude, rough, and inferior culinary ware that would not have inspired anyone to imitate it. Maria and Julian's early pieces were characterized by small, simple shapes and simple geometric designs, and again (it must be stressed) always in polychrome (Figures 7.7-7.18). She did not begin making larger pieces until about 1915.

Around 1912, Maria and Julian did start producing plain polished Blackware, but the inspiration for this form did not come from the Pajarito Plateau. San Ildefonso, San Juan, and especially Santa Clara pueblos had a long tradition of Blackware with which Maria was familiar, and they simply adopted a form already being made by the other potters. In their unique way, however, they refined the form, achieving a more highly polished and lustrous finish that proved more saleable to outsiders. In 1919, Maria and Julian made a true discovery with the development of Black-on-black ware (as already discussed in Chapter Three). This was the form that would achieve international fame for the couple and that would be emulated by the other potters of San Ildefonso, and subsequently Santa Clara and other pueblos.

Gunmetal Firing. In the original edition, in the discussion of Black-on-black ware firing techniques (page 48), a quotation was taken from Kenneth Chapman that stated, "For the best black color, the firing must be cool. In fact, if the firing temperature exceeds 650° C., although the ware is much harder and more durable, the resulting shrinkage of the slip produces a greyish gunmetal surface that is less attractive." The author

TYPICAL PIECES OF MARIA AND JULIAN'S EARLY WORK

Figures 7.7-7.9   Typical examples of Maria and Julian's work from the period 1907 to 1915.
Kenneth M. Chapman Archives, courtesy School of American Research, Santa Fe, New Mexico.

TYPICAL EXAMPLES OF MARIA AND JULIAN'S EARLY POTTERY

Figure 7.10 Polychrome jar; stepped key, floral, and curvilinear designs, 3½" x 7½". Unsigned. Dated c. 1915 by Kenneth M. Chapman. School of American Research Catalog No. IAF2012.

Figure 7.11 Polychrome bowl; floral, geometric, and cloud designs, 2¼" x 7¼". Unsigned. Dated 1918 by K. M. Chapman. School of American Research Catalog No. IAF1377.

Figure 7.12 Polychrome prayer meal bowl; cloud, rain, kiva, and corn designs, 3¾" x 6¼". Unsigned. Dated 1914-1915 by K. M. Chapman. School of American Research Catalog No. IAF1931.

Figure 7.13 Polychrome dipper (or ladle); cloud and lightning arrow designs, 4" x 5". Unsigned. Dated 1915 by K. M. Chapman. School of American Research Catalog No. IAF2118.

Figure 7.14 Polychrome bowl; curvilinear and stepped designs, 2¾" x 7". Signed: Marie. Dated 1923 by K. M. Chapman. School of American Research Catalog No. IAF2347.

Figure 7.15 Polychrome bowl; eight-pointed star and cloud designs, 3½" x 10½". Unsigned. Dated 1915 by K. M. Chapman. School of American Research Catalog No. IAF1907.

Figure 7.16 Polychrome jar; geometric and curvilinear designs, 4⅜" x 8½". Signed: Marie. Dated 1923 by K. M. Chapman. School of American Research Catalog No. IAF2349.

Figure 7.17 Polychrome bowl; wing, stepped, and checkerboard designs, 3½" x 10½". Unsigned. Dated c. 1916 by K. M. Chapman. School of American Research Catalog No. IAF1379.

Figure 7.18 Polychrome bowl; geometric and cloud designs, 3" x 8¾". Signed: Marie San Ildefonso, NM. Dated 1923 by K. M. Chapman. School of American Research Catalog No. IAF2348.

All photographs courtesy School of American Research, Santa Fe, New Mexico.

assumed the reader would make the distinction between the dull gray from over-firing that Mr. Chapman was discussing and the highly polished and lustrous gunmetal firing that Popovi Da produced at a later period. This point is brought up here to clarify some confusion that seems to have resulted from Mr. Chapman's quotation.

The Hollenback Storage Jar, Figure 3.7 (page 38) is a new photograph of a different pot. The attribution of the vessel included in the first edition as being made by Maria and Julian Martinez was incorrect. The story of who might be the actual potter is an interesting one.

The fact that this vessel has a San Ildefonso stone-polished white slip and a stone-polished red rim helps greatly in dating, as very little San Ildefonso stone-polished white slip was used after about 1905, when Cochiti slip was introduced. The red rim was all but abandoned by 1910 in favor of a black-painted rim, also borrowed from the Keres. The nice balance of black and red in the design indicates the jar could not have been made much before 1900, when the use of red was more cautious and hesitant.

Considering the characteristics of this piece—shape and style as well as painting style and quality—the most likely candidates as makers would be Dominguita Pino, who was best known for her Black-on-red ware, or the well-known husband-and-wife team of Florentino and Martina Montoya. The shape and style of the finished piece does not seem quite right for Florentino and Martina Montoya, however.* There is not enough documented pottery by Dominguita, particularly in Polychrome, to determine the maker solely by studying the piece.

Probably the best evidence we have as to the maker is the identification of the jar by Tomasita Montoya Sanchez as being the work of her grandmother, Dominguita Pino (1860-1948). In fact, her evidence seems quite conclusive. Tomasita is the eldest daughter of Tonita Martinez Montoya Roybal and the granddaughter of Dominguita Pino (Martinez). She remembers this pottery vessel quite well from her youth, when it occupied a place in their house. As she relates the story, on the occasion of her marriage in 1937, her mother, Tonita, determined they would have to sell the jar in order to pay for the wedding. She recalls Tonita saying at the time that she hated to sell the pottery because it had been made by her mother, but the jar was taken to Santa Fe and sold to a patroness, Amelia Hollenback. As further evidence, Tomasita produced a photograph taken circa 1924 of her grandmother with the storage jar in front of the family home (page 134).

133

Dominguita Pino Martinez sitting with her large storage jar, her husband Santiago Martinez, and her grandson J.D. Roybal. Photograph c. 1924.

Tomasita further identifies the decorator of the storage jar as being Dominguita's son, Crescencio Martinez (1879-1918). Considering the painting style and quality of execution used in the adaptation of the nineteenth-century Acoma design, Crescencio would be one of the few prior to Julian able to produce such a piece. It is known that this foremost watercolorist decorated pottery prior to 1910, painting the work of his mother, Dominguita Pino; his wife and Maria's eldest sister, Maximiliana Montoya Martinez; his sister, Tonita Montoya Roybal; and also Maria Martinez, in the early years of her career.

No matter who the maker and decorator were, this storage jar is an example of San Ildefonso pottery art at its finest. Not only is it magnificent for its sheer size, but it is the work of a master-potter in form and technique, and of an adept and skilled artist, who used the surface of the vessel as his canvas.

134

The Maria Exhibition at the Millicent Rogers Museum. Courtesy The Millicent Rogers Museum, Taos, New Mexico.

The Millicent Rogers Museum. In 1982 the Millicent Rogers Museum in Taos, New Mexico, acquired Popovi Da's private collection of Maria's pottery, which includes some of her finest and most important works. This collection has provided the nucleus for the museum's outstanding and unique collection, which includes pottery of Popovi Da, Tony Da, Santana and Adam, Barbara Gonzales, and other family members.

Through the generosity of the Da family, Maria's personal possessions and working materials are on exhibit as well. These pieces include Maria's tools used in pottery-making, such as gourds, polishing stones, sifters, and scrapers. There is also a series of photographs by Laura Gilpin, demonstrating the steps of firing pottery. Eight clay pots made by Maria illustrate the stages of building and finishing a jar. There are experimental pieces made by Maria and Popovi. Maria's personal possessions, the stool on which she worked, jewelry, and clothing, are part of the exhibit, as well. Maria's many awards, medals, and citations are also on display. All of these pieces are of great interest and historical significance and contribute to the total museum experience, but the heart of the exhibit is in the pottery itself.

The museum has since built a new facility to house this collection, making it the finest of Maria's work permanently accessible to the general public.

Signatures. Since the first publication of this volume, a rare signature—"Marie Poveka"—by Maria has been found in a private collection. It

135

Left to right: Figure 7.19 Polished Red Bowl (c. 1955). 3″ x 10″. Signature: Marie Poveka. Figure 7.20 Marie Poveka. Both pieces courtesy Santa Fe East Collection, Santa Fe, New Mexico. Photographs by Herbert Lotz.

appears on the bottom of a Polished Red open bowl, circa 1955 (Figures 7.19, 7.20); this piece, which is in the Santa Fe East Collection, was included in the Maria Retrospective at the Wheelwright Museum in 1980. The bowl measures 10 inches at the widest diameter and is 3 inches high. This would have appeared at the time Maria was changing her signature from "Marie" to "Maria," which, as has been previously stated, occurred in 1956 when she began working with Popovi Da. This would have probably been one of the rare pieces to carry the "Marie Poveka" signature. No other pieces with this signature have been seen by this author. It would have also been one of the first to have used "Poveka" since the early pieces in 1918 that were discussed in Chapter Four.

Additional information has also been found regarding the signature on the pottery of Popovi Da. It has been previously recorded that the first piece signed "Popovi" (alone) appeared in 1965. A small bowl with the feather design has since been found in the collection of Jerry McClelland of Arlington, Virginia, with the firing date of September 1962. The 1965 date now stands corrected.

The legacy of Maria is a significant one. In the first part of the twentieth century, Pueblo pottery-making was in serious decline and economic conditions at the pueblos were at an all-time low. There were many who predicted a total demise of the art. Then came Maria and Julian Martinez, who by their example were the key figures in leading a pottery revival.

Their influence was quickly felt at San Ildefonso, but soon extended to the other pueblos as well, and pottery-making once again became an important economic product. Edgar L. Hewett felt so strongly about the importance of Maria's influence that he stated:

> If Maria Martinez, famous potter of San Ildefonso, for any of the reasons that cause ladies to change residence—matrimony, kidnapping, elopement, and so on—should have been transplanted to Zuni, it is safe to say that there would have resulted a revolution in the ceramics of that community (Hewett 1938, revised 1953:127).

Today, Maria's legacy is no less important. Pottery-making has become the single most important source of income at most of the pueblos, and its importance is such that most potters are now at an income level that can be described as affluent. Today's prices are a far cry from those of just a few years ago, when a major piece of pottery could be purchased at a relatively low price. Perhaps even more important, Maria and Julian saved an important part of the American cultural heritage from extinction.

Members of Maria's family carry on the tradition. Most important, of course, are Santana and Adam, who continue the Black-on-black tradition and produce fine pieces. Adam and Santana's granddaughters, Barbara Gonzales and Kathleen Sanchez, have become important potters, working in more contemporary sgraffito style. Daughter-in-law Pauline Martinez is actively carrying on the Black-on-black tradition and granddaughter Beverly Martinez also does pieces in Black-on-black.

Maria's niece, Carmelita Dunlap, works in Polychrome, Black-on-black, and Buff-on-red. Nephew Albert Vigil, working with his wife, Josephine, are producing fine wares in Black-on-black, but are best known for their Buff-on-red.

Gilbert Atencio, Helen Gutierrez, and Angelita Sanchez, close relatives as well, are doing important work. Gilbert has worked in Polychrome; Helen is well known for her Buff-on-red, Black-on-black, and Sienna wares; Angelita works in Black-on-black.

There are potters from other San Ildefonso families who continue to work in the San Ildefonso tradition. Perhaps best known is Blue Corn, whose work includes Black-on-black, Buff-on-red, Polychrome, and sometimes innovative uses of micaceous clay. Florence Naranjo has been creating Black-on-black for many years. Margaret Lou Gutierrez, daughter of Tonita Roybal, does very nice Black-on-black ware. Tse Pe, continuing the tradition of his late mother and outstanding potter, Rose Gonzales, does pieces in sgraffito and carved ware. Dora Tse Pe Pena, working in a similar vein, does some excellent pottery. Russell Sanchez and Juan Tafoya each are known for their sgraffito, although Juan also works in Black-on-black.

Although she learned pottery-making on her own, Blue Corn feels Maria was an important influence. "One time she told me to keep up with my pottery and to stay with it, and pray every time when I go for some clay, the white clay and the red clay. To know her, she was a really good lady." In discussing Maria's importance in pottery-making to other potters, Blue Corn noted, "It is important since she's the lady that made pottery first. Well, there were other ladies that were making pottery before her, but she was the one that went out to sell her wares and people have known her all over the world. . . . It was inspiring for me to see her make pottery and she was known and she was a great lady."*

Maria was not selfish with her work. She shared her knowledge and skills and never considered herself better than any of the other potters. In her own mind, she was simply one of many San Ildefonso potters. Such is the legacy of Maria Martinez.

Figure 7.21   San Ildefonso Mythical Bird. Watercolor by Julian Martinez. 20" x 26." Private Collection. Photograph by Herbert Lotz.

*Personal interview

NOTES TO THE CHAPTERS

INDIAN POTTERY AND INDIAN VALUES

1. Popovi Da, "Indian Pottery and Indian Values," *Exploration 1970*, pp. 2–7.

CHAPTER ONE

1. Alice Marriott, *María: The Potter of San Ildefonso*, p. xi.

CHAPTER TWO

1. Kenneth M. Chapman, *Pueblo Indian Pottery*, Vol. I, pp. 5–6.
2. James Stevenson, "Illustrated Catalogue of the Collections Obtained from the Indians of New Mexico and Arizona in 1880," *Second Annual Report, Bureau of American Ethnology*, p. 461.
3. Ibid., pp. 432–33.
4. Kenneth M. Chapman, *The Pottery of San Ildefonso Pueblo*, p. xi.
5. Ibid., p. 33.
6. Alfred Kidder, in Introduction to *Pueblo Pottery Making*, by Carl E. Guthe, p. 12.
7. Herbert J. Spinden, "The Making of Pottery at San Ildefonso," *The American Museum Journal*, p. 194.
8. Larry Frank and Francis H. Harlow, *Historic Pottery of the Pueblo Indians, 1600–1880*, p. 9.
9. Ibid., p. 35.
10. Ruth Bunzel, *The Pueblo Potter*, p. 82.
11. Kidder, in Introduction to *Pueblo Pottery Making* by Carl E. Guthe, p. 13.

CHAPTER THREE

1. Ruth Bunzel, *The Pueblo Potter*, p. 58.
2. Ibid., p. 82.
3. Alfred V. Kidder, Introduction to *Pueblo Pottery Making* by Carl E. Guthe, pp. 13–14.
4. Carl E. Guthe, *Pueblo Pottery Making*, p. 61.
5. Kenneth M. Chapman, *The Pottery of San Ildefonso Pueblo*, pp. 29, 30.

6. Alice Marriott, *María, The Potter of San Ildefonso*, p. 218.
7. *El Palacio*, July, 1920, p. 217.
8. Kenneth M. Chapman, *The Pottery of San Ildefonso Pueblo*, pp. 34-35.
9. Ibid., p. 34.
10. Carl E. Guthe, *Pueblo Pottery Making*, p. 24.
11. Kenneth M. Chapman, *The Pottery of San Ildefonso Pueblo*, p. 35.
12. Carl E. Guthe, *Pueblo Pottery Making*, p. 66.
13. Ruth Bunzel, *The Pueblo Potter*, p. 88.
14. Ibid., p. 66.
15. Kenneth M. Chapman, *The Pottery of San Ildefonso Pueblo*, p. 30.
16. Alfred V. Kidder, *An Introduction to the Study of Southwestern Archaeology*, p. 42.
17. Ruth Bunzel, *The Pueblo Potter*, p. 5.
18. Odd S. Halseth, "The Revival of Pueblo Pottery Making," p. 136.

CHAPTER FOUR

1. Nancy Fox, "Poveka: A Signature of Maria Martinez," p. 261.
2. Ibid., pp. 260–61.
3. Ibid., p. 261.
4. Alice Marriott, *María: The Potter of San Ildefonso*, p. 227.
5. Popovi Da, Statement on file at the Museum of New Mexico, and personal communication c. 1970.
6. Ruth Bunzel, *The Pueblo Potter*, pp. 66–67.
7. William Whitman, *The Pueblo Indians of San Ildefonso*, pp. 114–15.

CHAPTER FIVE

1. "Machines and Artists," *The Masterkey*, p. 156.

CHAPTER SIX

1. Carl E. Guthe, *Pueblo Pottery Making*, p. 75.

Popovi Da painting a feather design with a yucca brush. Photograph by Peter Dechert.

BIBLIOGRAPHY

Arizona Highways. Vol. L, No. 5, May, 1974.

Austin, Mary. *Indian Pottery of the Rio Grande.* Pasadena: Esto Publishing Co., 1934.

Bahti, Tom. *Southwestern Indian Arts and Crafts.* Flagstaff, Arizona: KC Publications, 1964.

————. *Southwestern Indian Tribes.* Flagstaff, Arizona: KC Publications, 1968.

Bacon, Lucy. "Indian Independence through Tribal Arts." *New Mexico,* Vol. X, No. 1, January, 1932, pp. 11-13, 44.

Batkin, Jonathan. *Pottery of the Pueblos of New Mexico 1700-1940.* Colorado Springs: The Tayor Museum of the Colorado Springs Fine Arts Center, 1987.

Blair, Mary Ellen and Laurence. *Margaret Tafoya: A Tewa Potter's Heritage and Legacy.* West Chester, Pennsylvania: Schiffer Publishing, Ltd., 1986.

Bunzel, Ruth. *The Pueblo Potter: A Study of Creative Imagination in Primitive Art.* New York: Columbia University Press, 1929. (Reprint: New York: Dover Publications, Inc., 1972.)

Burton, Henrietta K. *The Re-establishment of the Indians in Their Pueblo Life through the Revival of Their Traditional Crafts: A Study in Home Extension Education.* New York: Teachers College, Columbia University, 1936.

Chapman, Kenneth M. *The Pottery of San Ildefonso Pueblo.* School of American Research Monograph No. 28. Albuquerque: University of New Mexico Press, 1970.

————. "Indian Pottery." *Introduction to American Indian Art,* Pt. II. New York: Exposition of Indian Tribal Arts, Inc., 1931, pp. 3-11.

————. *Pueblo Indian Pottery,* Vol. I. Nice, France: C. Szwedzicki, 1933.

————. *Pueblo Pottery of the Post-Spanish Period.* Laboratory of Anthropology, General Series, Bulletin No. 4. Santa Fe, 1938.

Colton, Harold S. *Potsherds: An Introduction to the Study of Prehistoric Southwestern Ceramics and Their Use in Historic Reconstruction.* Flagstaff, Arizona: Northern Arizona Society of Science and Art, 1953.

Curtis, Edward S. *The North American Indian,* Vol. 17. Norwood, Massachusetts: Plimpton Press, 1926.

Da, Popovi. "Chronology of Signatures." A statement on file at the Museum of New Mexico, Laboratory of Anthropology, 1969.

————. "Indian Pottery and Indian Values." *Exploration 1970.* Santa Fe: School of American Research, 1970, pp. 2-7.

————. "Indian Values." *The Quarterly of the Southwestern Association on Indian Affairs, Inc.* Vol. 6, Spring, 1969, No. 2, pp. 15-19. (Reprint: Vol. 12, Summer, 1977, No. 2, pp. 2-6.)

Douglas, Frederick H. *Pueblo Indian Pottery Making.* Denver Art Museum, Department of Indian Art, Leaflet No. 6, Denver, 1930.

————. *Modern Pueblo Pottery Types.* Denver Art Museum, Department of Indian Art, Leaflet Nos. 53 and 54, Denver, 1933.

————. *Pottery of the Southwestern Tribes.* Denver Art Museum, Department of Indian Art, Leaflet Nos. 69 and 70, Denver, 1935.

Douglas, Frederick H. and D'Harnoncourt, Rene. *Indian Art of the United States.* New York: Museum of Modern Art, 1941.

Dunn, Dorothy. *American Indian Painting of the Southwest Plains Areas.* Albuquerque: University of New Mexico Press, 1968.

Dutton, Bertha P. *Indians of the American Southwest*. Englewood Cliffs, New Jersey: Prentice Hall, Inc., 1975.

El Palacio, Vol. VIII, Nos. 7 and 8. Santa Fe, New Mexico: Museum of New Mexico, July, 1920, p. 217.

Ellsberg, Helen. *Western Collector*. May, 1969, pp. 206-211.

Farrington, William. *Prehistoric and Historic Pottery of the Southwest: A Bibliography*. Santa Fe, New Mexico: Sunstone Press, 1975.

Field, Clark. *Indian Pottery of the Southwest: Post Spanish Period*. Tulsa, Oklahoma: Philbrook Art Center, 1963.

Fine, Roberta Ross. "The Legacy of Maria Martinez." *The Santa Fean Magazine*. Vol. 8, No. 9, October 1980, pp. 30-34.

Fox, Nancy. "Poveka, A Signature of Maria Martinez." *Collected Papers in Honor of Marjorie F. Lambert*. Papers of the Archaeological Society of New Mexico: 3. Albuquerque: Albuquerque Archaeological Society Press, 1976, pp. 259-64.

Frank, Larry, and Harlow, Francis H. *Historic Pottery of the Pueblo Indians, 1600-1880*. Boston, Massachusetts: New York Graphic Society Ltd., 1974.

Gifford, E. W. *Pottery Making in the Southwest*. Publications in American Archaeology and Ethnology, Vol. 23. Berkeley: University of California, 1928, pp. 353-73.

Gilpin, Laura. *The Pueblos: A Camera Chronicle*. New York: Hastings House, 1941.

Goddard, Pliny Earle. *Pottery of the Southwestern Indians*. New York: American Museum of Natural History, 1931.

Gridley, Marion E. *American Indian Women*. New York: Hawthorn Books, Inc., 1974.

Guthe, Carl E. *Pueblo Pottery Making: A Study at the Village of San Ildefonso*. New Haven: Yale University Press, 1925.

Halseth, Odd S. "The Revival of Pueblo Pottery Making." *El Palacio*. Vol. XXI, No. 6, September 15, 1926, pp. 135-54.

Harlow, Francis H. *Matte Paint Pottery of the Tewa, Keres and Zuni Pueblos*. Santa Fe, New Mexico: Museum of New Mexico, 1973.

Hawley, Florence M. "Field Manual of the Prehistoric Southwestern Pottery Types." Albuquerque: University of New Mexico Bulletin, Revised November 1, 1950.

Hewett, Edgar L. *Antiquities of the Jemez Plateau*, Bulletin 32, Bureau of American Ethnology. Washington: Government Printing Office, 1906.

—————. *Les Communantés Anciens dans le Désert Américain*. Genève, Librarie Kündig, 1908.

—————. *Pajarito Plateau and Its Ancient People*. Albuquerque: University of New Mexico Press, 1938.

Hodge, Zahrah Preble. "Marie Martinez: Indian Master Potter." *Southern Workman*. Vol. 62, No. 5, 1933, pp. 213-15.

Howard, Richard M. "Contemporary Pueblo Indian Pottery." *Ray Manley's Southwestern Indian Arts and Crafts*. Tucson: Ray Manley Photography, Inc., 1975, pp. 33-52.

Hyde, Hazel. *Maria Making Pottery*. Santa Fe: Sunstone Press, 1973.

Jacka, Jerry, and Gill, Spencer. *Pottery Treasures*. Portland: Graphics Arts Center Publishing Co., 1976.

Kidder, Alfred V. *An Introduction to the Study of Southwestern Archaeology*. Papers of the Phillips Academy Southwestern Expedition, No. 1. New Haven: Yale University Press, 1924.

—————. *The Pottery of Pecos: The Dull-Paint Wares:* Vol. I. Papers of the Phillips Academy Southwestern Expedition, No. 5. New Haven: Yale University Press, 1931.

—————. *Pottery of the Pajarito Plateau and of Some Adjacent Regions in New Mexico*. Lancaster, Pennsylvania: American Anthropological Association, 1915.

Lambert, Marjorie F. *Pueblo Indian Pottery: Materials, Tools and Techniques*. Santa Fe, New Mexico: Museum of New Mexico Press, 1966.

Letterhouse, M. D. "Revival of Tribal Arts as a Factor in Pueblo Economic Independence." *Mission Fields at Home*, Vol. 4, Nos. 10-11, July-August, 1932, pp. 150-52.

Lyon, Dennis. "The Polychrome Plates of Maria and Popovi." *American Indian Art Magazine*, Vol. 1, No. 2, Spring, 1976, pp. 76-79.

"Machines and Artists." *The Masterkey.* Vol. VIII, No. 5, September, 1934. Los Angeles: Southwest Museum, p. 156.

"Maria: The Potter from San Ildefonso." *Artists of the Rockies,* Vol. 1, No. 2, Spring, 1974, pp. 20-24.

"Maria." *Exploration 1979.* Santa Fe: School of American Research, 1979, pp. 20-21.

Marriott, Alice. *María: The Potter of San Ildefonso.* Norman, Oklahoma: University of Oklahoma Press, 1948.

"Martinez, Maria Antonita." *Who's Who of American Women.* Eighth Edition, 1974-1975. St. Louis: Von Hoffman Press, Inc., p. 613.

McGreevy, Susan Brown. *Maria: The Legend, the Legacy.* Santa Fe: Sunstone Press, 1982.

Mera, H. P. "Wares Ancestral to Tewa Polychrome." *Laboratory of Anthropology Technical Series Bulletin No. 4.* Santa Fe, 1932.

——————. "Style Trends of Pueblo Pottery in the Rio Grande and Little Colorado Cultural Areas from the Sixteenth to the Nineteenth Century." *Laboratory of Anthropology Memoirs.* Vol. 3. Santa Fe, 1939.

Monthan, Guy and Doris. *Art and Indian Individualists.* Flagstaff, Arizona: Northland Press, 1975.

Nelson, Mary Carroll. *Maria Martinez.* Minneapolis, Minnesota: Dillon Press, 1972.

Oppelt, Norman. *Southwestern Pottery: An Annotated Bibliography and List of Types and Wares.* Occasional Publications in Anthropology, Archaeology Series, No. 7. Greeley, Colorado: Museum of Anthropology, University of Northern Colorado, 1976.

Peterson, Susan. *The Living Tradition of Maria Martinez.* Tokyo: Kodansha International, 1977.

Pottery of San Ildefonso: Membership Exhibit. Santa Fe, New Mexico: School of American Research, 1971.

Saunders, Charles Francis. "The Ceramic Art of the Pueblo Indians." *International Studio,* Vol. 41, No. 161, 1910, pp. 66-70.

Seven Families in Pueblo Pottery. Maxwell Museum of Anthropology. Albuquerque: University of New Mexico Press, 1974.

Shepard, Anna D. *Ceramics for the Archaeologist.* Washington, D.C.: Carnegie Institution of Washington, Publication 609, 1965.

Snodgrass, Jeanne O. *American Indian Painters: A Biographical Directory.* New York: Museum of the American Indian: Heye Foundation, 1968.

Spinden, Herbert J. "The Making of Pottery at San Ildefonso." *The American Museum Journal,* Vol. XI, No. 6, pp. 192-96.

Spivey, Richard L. "Pottery." *Arizona Highways: Indian Arts and Crafts.* Ed.: Clara Lee Tanner. Phoenix: Arizona Highways, 1976, pp. 100-31.

——————. "Signed in Clay." *El Palacio.* Vol. 86, No. 4, Winter 1980-81, pp. 8-9.

Stevenson, James. "Illustrated Catalogue of the Collections Obtained from the Indians of New Mexico and Arizona in 1880." *Second Annual Report, Bureau of American Ethnology,* Smithsonian Institution, 1880-81. Washington, D.C.: U.S. Government Printing Office, pp. 429-65.

Tanner, Clara Lee. *Southwest Indian Painting: A Changing Art.* Tucson: University of Arizona Press, 1973.

——————. *Southwest Indian Craft Arts.* Tucson: University of Arizona Press, 1968.

Toulouse, Betty. "Pueblo Pottery Traditions: Ever Constant, Ever Changing." *El Palacio.* Vol. 82, No. 3, Fall, 1976, pp. 14-47.

——————. "Maria: The Right Woman at the Right Time." *El Palacio.* Vol. 86, No. 4, Winter 1980-81, pp. 3-7.

Underhill, Ruth. *Pueblo Crafts.* Lawrence, Kansas: Haskell Institute, 1944.

Whitman, William. *The Pueblo Indians of San Ildefonso: A Changing Culture.* Columbia University Contributions to Anthropology No. 34. New York: Columbia University Press, 1947.

Wilson, Olive. "The Survival of an Ancient Art." *Art and Archaeology.* Vol. 9, No. 1, Jan. 1920, pp. 24-29.

Wormington, H. M., and Arminta, Neal. *The Story of Pueblo Pottery.* Museum Pictorial No. 2. Denver: Denver Museum of Natural History, 1951.

GENEALOGY

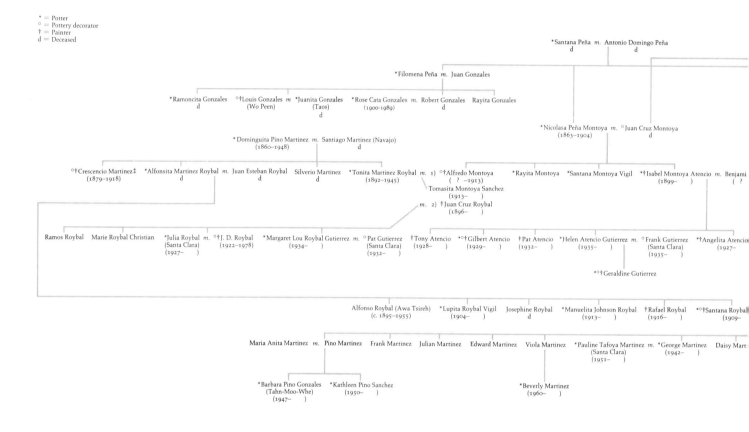

‡Crescencio Martinez is shown twice: as son of Domingita and Santiago Martinez and husband of Maximiliana Martinez.

144

Crucita Sanchez Montoya *m.* Juan Jose Montoya
d   d

*Luisita Peña Martinez *m.* Santiago Martinez
d   d

Reyes Peña Montoya *m.* Tomas Montoya
(? –1909)

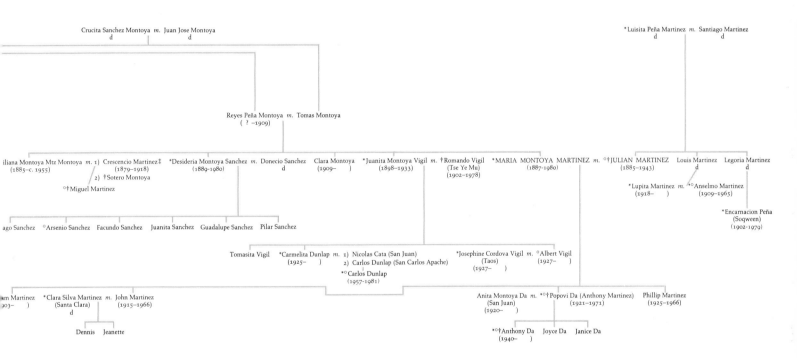

iliana Montoya Mtz Montoya *m.* 1) Crescencio Martinez‡ *Desideria Montoya Sanchez *m.* Donecio Sanchez   Clara Montoya   *Juanita Montoya Vigil *m.* †Romando Vigil   *MARIA MONTOYA MARTINEZ *m.* °†JULIAN MARTINEZ   Louis Martinez   Legoria Martinez
(1885–c. 1955)   (1879–1918)   (1889-1980)   d   (1909–)   (1898–1933)   (Tse Ye Mu)   (1887-1980)   (1885–1943)   d   d
                         2) †Sotero Montoya   (1902–1978)
        °†Miguel Martinez

*Lupita Martinez *m.* *°Anselmo Martinez
(1918–)   (1909–1965)

*Encarnacion Peña
(Soqween)
(1902-1979)

ago Sanchez   °Arsenio Sanchez   Facundo Sanchez   Juanita Sanchez   Guadalupe Sanchez   Pilar Sanchez

Tomasita Vigil   *Carmelita Dunlap *m.* 1) Nicolas Cata (San Juan)   *Josephine Cordova Vigil *m.* °Albert Vigil
                 (1925–)   2) Carlos Dunlap (San Carlos Apache)   (Taos)   (1927–)
                 *°Carlos Dunlap   (1927–)
                 (1957-1981)

m Martinez   *Clara Silva Martinez *m.* John Martinez   Anita Montoya Da *m.* *°†Popovi Da (Anthony Martinez)   Phillip Martinez
903–)   (Santa Clara)   (1915–1966)   (San Juan)   (1921–1971)   (1925–1966)
                                         d   (1920–)

             Dennis   Jeanette   *°†Anthony Da   Joyce Da   Janice Da
                                                                       (1940–)

145

Maria's and Julian's workroom with pottery in various stages of completion.

INDEX

Maria's hands. Photograph by Laura Gilpin.

But maybe God and the Great Spirit gave me (she claps her hands) that work [the hands to make pottery] . . . The spirit of the ones that passed away told me to love one another while we are on this earth. That's what God had told me, to keep it in my heart to love one another.

It's part of my work so that some day I could take it along with me. [The pottery she has made will stay here on this earth, but what goes into making them she will take along with her after death.]

I was never selfish with my work, for what God gave me. And so I help everybody. I used to teach at the government school in Santa Fe, the younger people from different pueblos. And now those ladies have . . . children, grandchildren, married. But some still come and visit me and thank me for what they learned from me. So I said, God gave me that hand, but not for myself, for all my people.

I just thank God because it's not only for me; it's for all the people. I said to my god, the Great Spirit, my Mother Earth gave me this luck. So I'm not going to keep it. I take care of our people. And I'm glad that those ladies learn and everything, and I'm happy.

MARIA